T0208257

FORMER

&

LATTER RAINS

Signs of Resounding Apostolic Revival

DR. VICTOR T. NYARKO

authorHOUSE®

AuthorHouse™
1663 Liberty Drive
Bloomington, IN 47403
www.authorhouse.com
Phone: 833-262-8899

Published by AuthorHouse 04/24/2023

ISBN: 979-8-8230-0410-7 (sc)
ISBN: 979-8-8230-0409-1 (e)

Library of Congress Control Number: 2023905267

Print information available on the last page.

PRESENTED TO

FROM

DATE

Other Exciting Books by the Author.

DIVINE EMPOWERMENT

This book is an exposition on the power of the efficacious blood of Jesus Christ, the legacy and empowerment it provided for the first Apostles, for today's believer in Jesus Christ and for all who will come after. It reveals the resources that God through Christ has made available and at our disposal for the successful accomplishment of the great commission. It also teaches the reader, how one can tap into these resources by believing it, claiming it, and possessing it.

ISBN9-781484-879832

A DISCONNECTED GENERATION

This book presents striking differences between the génération of Moses and the génération of Joshua. Although Joshua's génération witnessed a glimpse of the miracles and wonder workings of God, they lacked a personal relationship with the God of their fathers and the God of Israel.

ISBN 1-59330-075-1

DEALING WITH REJECTION

Rejection of one kind or another is inevitable throughout ones' life; therefore, any tool that can be acquired to help deal with it should be a welcome choice. In this book, Dr. Nyarko presents the key elements that lead to the feeling of rejection and how to deal with rejection from a biblical perspective.
ISBN1-59330-471-4

BEAUTY FOR ASHES

It has been the church's traditionn to think that great revival could be sparked by extensive advertising, putting up the right preacher and playing the right music. If these are true ingredients for revival, then John the Baptist' revival which ignited and blazed a trail in the desolate and obscure wilderness of Judea wouldn't have had the impact it did. On the contrary, out of the ashes of repentance comes revival, refreshing rrestitution and restoration.
ISBN 1-59330-605-9

WHERE ARE THE FATHERS

 The lack of fathers at home has been one of society's greatest dilemmas of our time. This book has a timely word from the Lord for everyone. God our father is calling all fathers through the pen of this godly author and father, back to the honorable and critical role of fatherhood. Get ready, read it, repent, and pass it on. **ISBN13:9781593302436**

KINGDOM WORSHIP

 Music is part of worship, but good music alone does not constitute worship. In this book, the various Hebrew words for 'praise' are described. It sheds light on the true meaning of worship and what the popular command 'Hallelujah' means in the praise and worship of God. It comes from the two Hebrew words *Halal* which is the most radical form of praise and *Yah* which is the short form for Jehovah. To worship God, goes far beyond being an act. It should be a personal encounter with God's presence which should lead to the worshipper, leaving His presence with fulfillment and gratification. In brief, this book focuses on what it means to halal (praise) God, who ought to Halal (praise) Him and where he ought to be Halal (praised). **ISBN 978-1-4984-3509-3**

THE PRODIGAL FATHER

What has become popularly but also erroneously referred to as the story of the 'prodigal son' is part of a larger revelation that Jesus wanted to show his church. This book then culminates with the distinction that our Lord Jesus makes between Sonship and servanthood in his vineyard parable about the servants and sons who were sent out by the Lord to work on his vineyard. Are all humanity Sons of God through procreation as many claims? Or is there a distinction between Kingdom-Sons and Kingdom-Servants of God? This book's approach to the story will leave you amused, instructed, enlightened, stirred up, and challenged, but not bored! **ISBN: 978-1-947349-23-0**

THE ORDER OF MELCHIZEDEK.

This book takes the reader on an intriguing and interesting journey into the life and person, of a strange and isolated but unique bible personage called Melchizedek, He appears momentarily on the scene of bible history with the great Patriarch Abraham and then disappears from the pages of history just as suddenly as he appeared. All other references in the bible about him is traced back to this one occasion. He is said to be without father, mother, nor descent, having neither beginning of days, nor end of life. So, the questions then is who was Melchizedek? In what ways does his priestly order align with the Lord Jesus and yet differs from the Aaronic order of

Priesthood? Why should Melchizedek, and he alone, of all the Old Testament characters be thought of in a way that defies human mortality? This book's approach to the life and person of Melchizedek will leave you amused, instructed, enlightened, stirred up, and challenged, but not bored!

ISBN: 978-1-947349-21-6

THE 4 DEGREES OF RELATIONSHIP

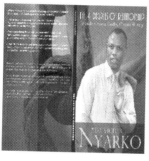 It's a matter of common knowledge that many of the headaches one goes through in life are because of bad associations. This book is about relationships, friendships, and associations, which is one of the key areas of our lives that we need to safeguard against. The key goal of this book is to teach the reader how to model their sphere of relationship after the pattern of Christ. We all, to some degree, have a sphere of association with other people who have the potential to impact the way we behave and the decisions we make in life. As the say goes, "no man is an Island," because we are all interconnected in one way or the other. That is why as humans, and by instinct people will put their lives in danger to save even strangers whom they do not know or have ever met.

One cannot underestimate the importance that Jesus placed on his associations because it is out of his associations that he chose the 12 disciples who he would later refer to as his friends. It was also out of the 12 disciples that he later chose the 3 disciples (Peter, James, and John) who became his inner circle and confidants. **ISBN: 9781642371093**
eISBN: 9781642371086

ANTIDOTE: HOW THE BLOOD OF THE LAMB GOES TO WORK FOR THE SINS OF HUMANITY

The subject of the blood of the Lamb is one of the most common topics of discussions, teachings, and sermons in the Christian circles. It was L.D. Bevan that said, "The subject of the blood of the Lamb of God and the mystery surrounding this subject, will ever remain one of the richest gold mines of evangelical thought. It occupies a central position in the doctrine of atonement, just like the phrase "God is Spirit" in John 4;24, occupies in relation to the doctrine of God." There is literally no Sunday that one would leave an Apostolic or Pentecostal church service without hearing the mention of the blood in one way or the other. Even casual, everyday conversations among born-again Believers, often triggers the usage or reference to the blood of Jesus. Many know about the fact that there is power in the blood of Jesus. Many are also very much aware of the redemptive power in the blood of the Lamb of God and how to plead that blood against the works of the enemy in a spiritual warfare. However, a good percentage of Believers in our churches today have very little or no knowledge about why the blood of Jesus is referred to as the Blood of the Lamb of God and the dynamics behind how the Blood of the Lamb goes to work on the behalf of humanity against sin or the devices of the devil. The purpose of this book is to unveil the revelation behind the central role the Blood of Jesus plays in our redemption and how its power goes into play against the sins of mankind.

ISBN: 9781642371093
eISBN: 9781642371086

BLOOD AND FIRE

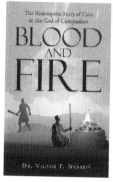

This book is about the biblical story of Cain and Abel, the first products of human procreation through Adam and Eve. This story is unique in that there are a couple of things done that were unknowns to human history. It is a story that although began with God's judgement against sinful human nature inherited through Adam and Eve, however, it ends with the powerful act of redemption that only comes from a God of second chances. This book is about the biblical story of Cain and Abel, the first products of human procreation through Adam and Eve. This story is unique in that there are a couple of things done that were unknowns to human history. It is a story that although began with God's judgement against sinful human nature inherited through Adam and Eve, however, it ends with the powerful act of redemption that only comes from a God of second chances.

ISBN : 1665507268

DEDICATION

This book is dedicated to my wife Joan Elaine,
my life-long companion, and best friend,

And To

Our three precious children Victoria, Vanya and
Joash who have dedicated their lives to God, been
an integral part of the work the Lord has called Joan
and I to do, and above all, have been godly examples
of the gospel of Jesus Christ to their generation.

Their lives are the delight of any godly parent.

CONTENTS

ACKNOWLEDGEMENT

Many thanks to the following people for your selfless service in making this book a possibility.

Editorial staff:
Felicia Amma Antwi (Ghana),

Photography:
Victoria Nyarko (VFWC)

Cover Design:
Author House Publishers

INTRODUCTION

Hosea 6:1–3

"Come, and let us return unto the LORD: for he hath torn, and he will heal us; he hath smitten, and he will bind us up.

2 After two days will he revive us: in the third day he will raise us up, and we shall live in his sight. 3 Then shall we know, if we follow on to know the LORD: his going forth is prepared as the morning; and he shall come unto us as the rain, as the latter and former rain unto the earth.

The *"two days"* of the prophecy of Hosea is believed by some Old Testament Theologians to be the 2,000 years that God has ordained for the grafting of the Gentiles into the "natural olive tree" that is represented by the nation of Israel. When Israel turned her back on God and away from the glorious Gospel of Jesus Christ and her failure to accept Him as the Messiah, blindness in part came upon the nation of Israel and some of her branches were cut off for the grafting in of the New Testament Gentile church until the fullness of the Gentiles is complete (Rom.11). When this comes to pass, then will the Gospel return to

Israel and then will God pour out both the *former* and *latter* rains upon Israel and as a result, her eyes shall be opened to the knowledge of the Lord Jesus Christ.

> *Forasmuch as the prophecy was directed towards the nation and people of Israel, the "Spiritual Israel", which is the New Testament Church, will also experience her own former and latter rains as testified by James in James 5:7–8.*

It is worth noting that the mention of the *rains* is associated with the *knowledge* of God.

"Be patient therefore, brethren, unto the coming of the Lord. Behold, the husbandman waiteth for the precious fruit of the earth, and hath long patience for it, until he receives the early and latter rain. Be ye also patient; stablish your hearts: for the coming of the Lord draweth nigh" (Jam.5:7–8).

Joel's Prophecy

According to the prophet Joel, there will come a terrible Day of the Lord upon the earth, but Israel is promised deliverance by the Lord. The Lord will send upon them the *former* and *latter* rains so that the nation will have plenty to eat as He restores all the years of destruction that He had put them through because of their disobedience and disbelieve. Then will God pour out His Spirit upon them as prophesy by Joel.

Joel 2:23

*Be glad then, ye children of Zion, and rejoice
in the LORD your God: for he hath given you
the former rain moderately, and he will cause
to come down for you the rain, the former rain,
and the latter rain in the first month.
24 And the floors shall be full of wheat, and
the fats shall overflow with wine and oil.
25 And I will restore to you the years that the locust
(i.e. the swarming locust) hath eaten, the cankerworm
(i.e. the crawling locust), and the caterpillar (i.e. the
consuming locust), and the palmerworm (i.e. the ravaging
locust), my great army which I sent among you.
26 And ye shall eat in plenty, and be satisfied,
and praise the name of the LORD your
God, that hath dealt wondrously with you:
and my people shall never be ashamed.
27 And ye shall know that I am in the midst of
Israel, and that I am the LORD your God, and
none else: and my people shall never be ashamed.*

28 *And it shall come to pass afterward, that I will pour out my spirit upon all flesh; and your sons and your daughters shall prophesy, your old men shall dream dreams, your young men shall see visions:*
29 *And also upon the servants and upon the handmaids in those days will I pour out my spirit.*
30 *And I will shew wonders in the heavens and in the earth, blood, and fire, and pillars of smoke.*
31 *The sun shall be turned into darkness, and the moon into blood, before the great and terrible day of the LORD come.*
32 *And it shall come to pass, that whosoever shall call on the name of the LORD shall be delivered: for in mount Zion and in Jerusalem shall be deliverance, as the LORD hath said, and in the remnant whom the LORD shall call.*

Notice what the 28th verse said? Until Israel is restored to the knowledge of the Lord, there will be no outpouring of the Holy Spirit upon them. But was the outpouring of the Spirit on the Day of Pentecost the *former* rain or the *latter* rain? That is an important question that needs to be answered and I will attempt to tackle this subject in the proceeding chapters of this book.

The Day of Pentecost

Concerning the outpouring of the Holy Spirit on the Day of Pentecost, let us look at how the apostle Peter used the words of the prophet Joel. It might be that there is some bearing between the two.

Acts 2:16

But this is that which was spoken by the prophet Joel;
17 And it shall come to pass in the last days, saith God,
I will pour out of my Spirit upon all flesh: and your sons
and your daughters shall prophesy, and your young men
shall see visions, and your old men shall dream dreams:
18 And on my servants and on my
handmaidens I will pour out in those days
of my Spirit; and they shall prophesy:
19 And I will shew wonders in heaven above, and signs
in the earth beneath; blood, and fire, and vapor of smoke:
20 The sun shall be turned into darkness,
and the moon into blood, before the great
and notable day of the Lord come:

> *We see is a precursor of the total fulfillment of Joel's prophecy that is still in the future, and the outpouring of the Holy Spirit on the Day of Pentecost could not be the former rain or the latter rain.*

21 And it shall come to pass, that whosoever shall call
on the name of the Lord shall be saved.

It is obvious that Peter's reference to the few verses of Joel's prophecy was not the complete fulfillment of all that Joel had prophesied concerning the restoration of Israel. What happened on the Day of Pentecost was only a foretaste of what the Jews will experience in the future when the Messiah comes for them. Remember that all who had the gift of the Holy Spirit on the Day of Pentecost were Jews. Furthermore, that Peter quoted Joel 2:28-32, which immediately follows Joel's prophecy of Israel's restoration by the Spirit of the Lord Joel 2:23-27 tells us of a complete fulfillment of a prophecy which is yet to come for Israel.

The First Advent of Christ saw the children of Israel restored to their homeland for some 480 years after the decree of Cyrus was issued, liberating them. The Word of the Gospel of the Lord was preached to them. Jesus Christ, the Husbandman, sowed the seeds, and for those who believed the word, they received the gift of the Holy Spirit on the Day of Pentecost and are sealed unto the day of redemption.

But when the Holy Spirit was given, what was it given for? Clearly, the Holy Spirit is not given to believers to speak in tongues, prophesy or to perform one of the many miraculous spiritual gifts because these are only signs to the unbelieving world. But the Spirit was given most importantly, to guide believers into all truth and to show them things yet to come, that Christ might be glorified as saith the Scriptures:

John 16:13

Howbeit when he, the Spirit of truth, is come, he will guide you into all truth: for he shall not speak of himself; but whatsoever he shall hear, that shall he speak, and he will shew your things to come.
14 *He shall glorify me: for he shall receive of mine and shall shew it unto you.*

The outpouring of the Holy Spirit on the Day of Pentecost was a testimony that life had come to those that had believed. It was given to guide the believers into all truth and to show them things yet to come. That is, the Spirit was showered upon them to cause them to grow and mature through the guidance of the Spirit in order to attain full stature by the revelation of the word. When the believers reach maturity then it is obvious that the Husbandman who is Christ, would then harvest His crop.

"Till we all come in the unity of the faith and of the knowledge of the Son of God, unto a perfect man, unto the measure of the stature of the fullness of Christ" **Ephesians 4:13**

Yes, Yahushua which is by interpretation; Joshua or Jesus sowed seeds and the Pentecostal rain came and the seeds began to sprout. As souls were added to the Church, the Spirit moved to teach them the truth and to show them things to come. He did these through the Ascension Gifts ministry or what is commonly known in the church as the five-fold ministry, namely

- *the prophetic,*
- *the evangelistic,*
- *the pastoral and*
- *the teaching ministries*
- *followed the apostolic ministry*

To give you a clearer picture, I would like to expound on the seasonal and theological relationships between the spring months and the fall months, between the spring festivals and the fall festivals. In ancient Israel there are the rains that pours in fall and the rains of the springtime. These are the literal former and latter rains respectively. It is important to understand this from an agricultural standpoint since Israel was predominantly an agricultural economy. Yet, there is a far more important concept that the Prophet Joel was trying to convey through his prophesy. As I navigate the chapters of this book, special emphasis will be placed on the various farming seasons that existed in the land of Israel, their theological relevance for today's believer and how they generally play into the divine providence of God and timetable of biblical prophecy.

CHAPTER 1

MISPLACED PRIORITIES

Observing God's creation, it is obvious for one to conclude that this super-genius creator God was up to something by the order He had set into creation. After creating the universe (the seen and unseen worlds, the flora and fauna), God set the big clock of nature into motion and order by separating the day from the night, the sun from the moon, and land from the sea.

Beside He placed all things he had created within their respective boundaries, so that;

- Although He did not set a fence between the land and the sea; yet each knows their boundaries and obey it.
- Although he did not tie a string to drag the sun away when the day is over and to bring in the moon and stars when the night is come; yet each body of light knows when to appear and when to disappear.
- Although the land space of earth is only one-third the size of the bodies of water, yet the bodies of

water do not overshadow the space covered by land. Likewise, the sun shines in the day, and it knows without being reminded that it must vacate its post to the moon by night. The vice versa applies to the moon in knowing that as the day breaks, it must give way to the sun.

I am giving all these examples to establish the fact that the great creator God had an ordained divine order behind everything He created. Hence, we see strings of these divine orders finely threaded throughout the pages of scripture. In this chapter, I will be exploring just a few theological examples of how some of these divine orders play out in the word of God.

A good example of God's divine order that I would like to highlight before I close the curtains on this subject can to found in **Obadiah 1:17-18**

> *"But upon mount Zion shall be deliverance, and there shall be holiness; and the house of Jacob shall possess their possessions.*
> *18 And the house of Jacob shall be a fire, and the house of Joseph a flame.….."*

A closer look at this scripture, reveals one of those divine orders in God's word. We often hear so much about the so-called 'prosperity gospel' that has invaded the standards of holiness in today's churches to the extent that if the preacher does not preach about prosperity; some people get offended and would not return to a particular church.

As a result, some has turned the true gospel of Jesus Christ into a "hand-me-down" gospel to suit their lustful desires and are passing it on to others; to the extent that many believers don't seek to live holy lives anymore. It is always about God is about to give you something or God is about to do something new in your life; but very little or nothing at all about God's desire for the well-being of your soul.

Meanwhile the bible says in **III John 1;2** that *"I wish above all things that thou mayest prosper and be in health even as thy soul prospereth"*

The prosperity of the believer must of course go together and hand in hand with the prosperity of his or her soul. Today however, it seems to be all about the outward prosperity which is temporal by the way; at the expense of your soul which is eternal. According to God's divine order however, God's abundant blessings cannot come upon us if we are living unholy and unrighteous lives which is obviously in contrast to the will of God for the believer.

So, the prophet Obadiah; in Obadiah 1;17; gives us an example of one of those divine orders when he says;

> *"But upon mount Zion shall be deliverance, and there shall be holiness; and the house of Jacob shall possess their possessions."*
>
> *18 And the house of Jacob shall be a fire, and the house of Joseph a flame....."*

If I got the order right, then it ought to be; deliverance

as the prerequisite for holiness and holy living then becomes the prerequisite for possessing God's abundant blessings; That means when one is not fully delivered from the vices of his or her sinful past and is still living under the shadows and influence of former conduct, habits and behaviors, holiness then takes a backseat, hence the fullness of God's blessings and its fulfillment cannot be released upon such lives. Despite this fact, it's surprising to me that there are some elements in today's church who don't believe in deliverance. They claim that once you accept Christ into your life every stronghold that you once dealt with in your life goes away automatically. I however strongly believe that there are some habits and behaviors that still needs to be dealt with even after one has accepted Christ into their lives and until those strongholds are destroyed ones' Christian life becomes nothing but a constant struggle that drives ones' life in cycles.

> *Strongholds do not just 'fly' away and vanish into the endless skies by some mysterious way. They need to be dealt with until one totally overcome.*

And so here again the divine order prevails, and that

is; one must be delivered, leading to holy living before God, in order for one to possess the fullness of God's blessings upon their lives. Remember I said *fullness* not partial.

If you follow the scripture in Obadiah 1;18 carefully, you would notice that it is only after deliverance, holiness, and the release of God's abundant blessing that the text says; **"the house of Jacob shall be a fire, and the house of Joseph a flame…."**.

Notice it is not before but rather after. That goes to affirm the role of God's divine order in the life of the New Testament believer.

I would like to close this chapter with one last example of God's divine order at play in the scriptures. This example has to do with the creation story as recorded in the book of Genesis. Notice that there are three key things that validates God's intended role for the male man that God had created. The male was created first, and there was an interlude of time before the female was made (no one knows how long this time is except God); However, what we do know is that there must be a reason why the male was created first. The male was created first because he was designed to be the foundation upon which the human family will rest.

> **"The LORD God took the man and put him in the Garden of Eden to work it and take care of it. And the LORD God commanded the man" (Gen. 2:15–16)**

Genesis 2:15 reveals that the first thing God gave the

male man (Adam) was not work, it was not a woman, and neither was it even instructions; It was God's own presence in Eden.

The word *"garden"* means something that's fenced-in or an enclosure. Therefore, Eden the Garden was God's incubator (enclosure) for this new offspring God had created called man. In essence, Eden is not necessarily a place per say; it's an atmosphere that's saturated with the presence of God. Notice therefore that God did not allow the man He had created to wander about in an attempt to find Eden (His Presence). Notice also that God did not leave Eden as an option for the male man either. Instead, God took the male He had created and intentionally place him there; That is a deliberate effort and action on the part of God in order to ensure that man was in the right environment necessary for his spiritual growth and nourishment.

> *When a man cannot function well as he is created to function, the fundamental problem is not lack of money or education or intelligence. It is lack of God's presence in his life.*

Therefore, for the male man, Eden which symbolizes God's presence is not an option; it's a requirement needed for the male to function well as created by God to function.

MONEY

When my wife and I got married we had no money. As the saying goes, we were as broke as a church mouse. It was the late Dr. Myles Monroe who once said; "If you are broke and I am broke we two make a bad company". Although we were broke financially and did not have much to live on, we were kept by the grace of God and by the love, care and respect we had for one another. We will buy one apple and take turns to bite on it because we couldn't afford two. And oh I would usually allow her to take a bite first because I would tell her as a joke that Eve first took a bite on the apple in the garden of Eden.

EDUCATION

In those days, I did not have all the array of educational qualifications I have today. When I went to college for my first degree, I was fascinated about rocks, so I majored in Geology to the dismay and displeasure of my parents who were eagerly looking forward for me to become a medical doctor or an engineer. But not having any of these was not a problem, because knowing my purpose as a male and as a husband, I was able to function without any of these luxuries of life.

Therefore, when a male cannot function well, the fundamental problem is that he is trying to function outside of the confines of Eden (which signifies the presence of God). But sadly the devil has blinded many men to think that; being "man-ly" or that ones' masculinity lies in staying away from God. That's why some men think being in church is a thing for women and children, and weeping before the Lord is a sign of weakness, but the devil is a liar because God's presence is the first and foremost thing that the male needs to validate his identity and function as a real male.

Hello gentlemen: I don't mean to offend anybody, but this is a synopsis of how real men should look like.

Real men love Jesus.

Real men love His word.

Real men love prayer.

Real men seek intimacy with God.

Real men love to be in God's presence.

And so here again, we see a clear-cut divine order.

- *GOD first gave the male his PRESENCE,*

> ***In essence, a man who doesn't love God's presence and who doesn't like to work doesn't deserve to have a woman (a wife).***

- *AND then he gave the male WORK*
- *AND then he gave the male a WOMAN*

Single Sisters are you listening? God has a word for you. When any brother approaches you about wanting your hand in marriage, this should be the litmus test or your check list to know whether they are real men or not.

– *Do they love God's presence?*
– *Do they love working for the Kingdom of God*
– *If the answer to these questions is "NO" then run for your life but if the answer is "YES" then they deserve your attention.*

And for the brothers who are already married, you are not off the hook either. If your answer to this question is a "NO" then you should count yourself very lucky to still have your wife by your side, because you don't deserve one if you don't love God's presence and if you don't like work. If you ever try to mess up with God's divine order, nothing will work well outside that order.

I would like to close this chapter with the same passage of scripture quoted at the introduction at the beginning of this book

> *6 Come, and let us return unto the Lord: for he hath torn, and he will heal us; he hath smitten, and he will bind us up*
>
> *2 After two days will he revive us: in the third day he will raise us up, and we shall live in his sight*
>
> *3 Then shall we know, if we follow on to know the Lord: his going forth is prepared as the morning; and he shall come unto us as the rain, as the latter and former rain unto the earth.* **HOSEA 6;1-3**

The kind of language like ***"for God hath torn, and God hath smitten"*** that signals the opposite of what one expects the good and caring heavenly father to do for his helpless children, sound very uncomfortable to read knowing that when we go to God; we do so with the expectation to be healed and not torn apart and to be bonded together and not smitten apart. But that simply goes to show that indeed, God rules in the affairs of men; it is He who tears apart, and it is He who heals; It is God that smite, and it is God that binds or heal the broken hearted.

Before there were ever physicians in the history of humanity; God said, *"I am the LORD that health thee"* (**Exo. 15;26**)

Again, God declared in Deuteronomy 32;39 that; *"I kill, and I make alive; I wound, and I heal"*

And so, would you say to yourself that because God said he kills and he wounds, you will not approach His presence.? No, that should not be the case. When God kills, he does so to bring newness of life, and when He wounds, he does so for those wounds to save us from a more detrimental circumstances in our lives.

As an example, several years ago, my wife was diagnosed with a very rear medical condition that her doctors said there is no cure for. As a result, her future health seems very unpromising and our little family at the time did not know what to do or where to turn to. However, in the process of time, her doctors decided that they will be performing surgery on her to remove a small gland situated around the chest by name thymoma gland. Their reason was that although the removal of this gland is not a cure and will not lead to a cure of the medical condition she was experiencing, medical sciences has discovered that for patients suffering from this condition who had those glands remove, they felt a little better. As a result, she went in for the surgery, only for the Doctors to discover after removing the glands that the gland itself was cancerous. This turned out to be a testimony because the cancerous thymoma gland was far more detrimental than the medical condition she was diagnose with which would have killed her in no time as compared to the medical condition that she could lived with. In other words, God brought this sickness her way so her life could be preserved from the far more detrimental medical condition of having to battle cancer in its final stage. This is a perfect example of how at times God inflict wounds in order to heal.

The scripture in Hosea 6:1-2 speaks of certain three days within which God says through his prophet Hosea that He will accomplish some things in the life of the people of Israel. While these three days in Hosea's prophecy may not be a literal three 24-hour days as we know and measure time today, because most often the Bible speaks in symbolic language. The three-days could however be any number of years apart from each other. It could be 100 years apart; 500 years apart or even 1000 years apart or even more than that. No one knows exactly how far apart these three '*prophetic days*' are from each other, however what is important to us and for which I will be focusing on in this book is not how far apart these three prophetic days are from each other but rather;

- *What is done or accomplished within these three days.*
- *And the order in which they are accomplished.*

> *Principles are very important in the study of God's word because God's word is based on precept upon precept and line upon line.*

The reason being that this is what establishes the biblical principle of divine order. Whiles the methods of doing things may change with time, principles as we all know, do not change with time. It is a matter of common experience that one can change the style of doing things without changing the principle behind.

There are certain three days on the calendar of humanity during which God will never fail nor change. That means if there exist any other days outside these three days, don't even count on God to sustain you because that will mean he will change on you and ultimately fail you. Those three days within which God can never fail nor change are mentioned on Hebrews 13:8 and they are yesterday, today, and forever.

Hebrews 13;8. *"Jesus Christ the same yesterday, and today, and forever."*

Hence, if God did not fail you yesterday, and will not fail you today, and forever, then it obviously implies that there are no other days left on human calendar for which He may fail or change because yesterday, today, and forever, put together encompasses the past, present, and future.

Notice in **Hosea 6:2** that the prophet mentions a second day and a third day in his prophesy. On the second day he said there shall be revival and on the third day there will be life and regeneration. Therefore, if there is a second day and a third day, then it obviously implies that there must be a first day. Yet the passage is silent about the first day.

Hence there are two questions that needs to be answered.

1. *Where is the reference of a first day in this passage of scripture?*
2. *What is the purpose of that first day?*

It is worth noting that the day-one or first day has to do with repentance, and it is clearly spoken of in the verse one although it is not labeled as day-one.

This imply God's divine order is repentance first, followed by revival and then new life and regeneration follows that. However, for most part, today's church has become the kind of church that speaks so much about revival, and all we often hear from the pulpits is.

- *God is about to do something great*
- *God is about to do this.*
- *God is about to do that.*

So, the popular rhetoric within today's church is "GOD IS ABOUT TO DO SOMETHING". What we hear for the most part is that God is always about to do yet we don't see much of the things we claim He is about to do because this statement has become a way of creating a hype and gearing people into empty promises and excitement.

When is God going to bring the revival we often claim He is about to do, and why is it tarrying for so long? The answer to these questions can be found in the same text. Notice in the text that revival does not come on day-one. It comes in day-two and only after God's people have fulfilled the prerequisite for revival that is mentioned in association with the first day and which is a call to repentance.

> *Just as there cannot be a day-two without a day-one; there also cannot be a revival without repentance. What we are dealing with today is a church that is promising abundance of rain while its' members have not yet repented; a church promising revival; while its members are wallowing in sin and worldliness; a church promising abundance of God's blessings; while its afraid of preach holiness without which no man shall see God.*

It is about time the church of today learn that the

prerequisite to the revival we have been eagerly seeking for doesn't come without repentance.

Notice from the text that it is only after the nation and its people had repented that God brought revival and consequently, the promise of abundant life and blessing.

> *"He will raise us up and then shall we continue to live in his presence".*

Also, it is not until after the third day that God promises abundance of rain. Whenever the church reverses the divine order in God's word, what we have at hand is a misplaced priority. That is why following God's divine order is so important. It is because it is connected to the blessing and wellness of the child of God.

And so, the Prophet says; *"6 Come, and let us return unto the Lord: for he hath torn, and he will heal us; he hath smitten, and he will bind us up"*

This is not the time for the church to be joking around. This is not the time for members of the body of Christ to be fighting one another. This is certainly not the time to be hiding our faces and pretending all is well. It is time for us to return unto God says the noble Prophet. Notice also that it was not until the third day that God promises abundance of rain, both the former and the latter rains together. Meaning, you can even claim to be in revival and not have abundant rain. You will have some rain, but it will only be in sporadic proportions instead of in double portions because repentance always ought to come first before a true and genuine revival.

I searched the 'strong concordance' for words that

align with revival, and listed below are some of the common words I came across in my search. I noticed that they are mostly those words that starts with **"re"**. Examples are as follows;

recover,

reactivate,

restore,

retrieve,

renew,

rebirth,

revitalize,

rejuvenate,

reawakening,

resurrect,

resurgence,

However, believe it or not, to my amusement, among the list was also the word 'repent' and I was wandering how that is possible.

However, repentance has become the very thing that the church of today and most of its members are shying away from because we have demonized that word even without first seeking to understand what it really means.

When the pastor or preacher calls for repentance at the altar; you will see people trying to hide their faces or look for the back door of the church to escape quietly as if they feel embarrassed by the call to repentance.

My amusement and search on the word *'repent'* led me to the following;

Repent; comes from two words put together

1) *RE= Return*

2) *PENT= The top-most part of a building.*

So, to be called to repentance simply means the Lord is calling us to get back to the topmost position where we truly belong in the first place. Therefore, repentance is not a word to shy away from but rather a command to embrace. I repent every morning during my early morning personal devotion time because by repenting; what I am saying to God is that; "please put me back to the top (pent) where I belong".

On the contrary, the church of today is going about revival in a reverse order. What we are hearing from some pulpits today is nothing but a reversed polarity and misplaced priority indeed. The prosperity gospel that has taken over many pulpits is causing preachers to go about.

- Promising rain while the church has not yet repented.
- Promising revival, while its members are wallowing in sin and worldliness.
- The church is promising abundance of God's blessings; while its afraid to preach holiness without which no man shall see God.

Instead of finding out the missing piece of the puzzle that fits into day-one of God's agenda, and which is to also serve as the pre-requisite to bring down true revival, instead, the church of today is caught up in empty hype and has become a church that talks a lot about revival but do little as far as pre-requisite of revival is concern. This is nothing but a misplaced priority.

CHAPTER 2

PRINCIPLE OF DESIRE

The King James Version, Psalm 65 reads:

> *"Thou visitest the earth* after thou hast made it to desire rain*"*
> *"Thou blessest the springing thereof"*
> *"Thou preparest them corn, when thou hast so provided for it"* (<u>*verse 9d, e*</u>).
> *"Thou waterest the ridges thereof...*
> *Thou makest it soft with showers."*

Based on the premises of divine order that has been established in chapter one, before revival comes to God's people, God first gives them the hunger and appetite for revival through genuine repentance. That's why the bible clearly states in Matthew 5: that it is only those who hunger and thirst after righteousness who shall be filled. If an individual or the church as a corporate body settles for the status quo and decide to go about God's business in their own way without a hunger and burning desire for the things of God, God will certainly not impose his presence on the church.

There certainly got to be a hunger and a thirst in order for a wave of revival to sweep over God's people. In line with divine order, the above passage of scripture teaches us that for the church to experience true revival, there must be some prerequisite. In line with that, the remarkable thing that nature teaches us is that before the rains come down after a prolong period of dryness, the earth opens its mouth by developing patches of cracks in the earth to receive rain. This natural phenomenon signifies the earth's desire for something that is urgently lacking, and which is needed for the earth to be productive. It is as though the pores are opened and the earth is longing to be filled with rain. As a result, the earth positions itself by opening its mouth in preparation to receive rain. The earth desires rain, as the scripture says here ***"Thou visitest the earth, and waterest it: thou greatly enrichest it with the river of God"*** [verse 9].

This is a great divine principle of God that we must first acknowledge in order to understand how God deals with His creation.

One of the great principles that God works upon is that He **"*satisfies the desire of every living thing*" [Psalm 145:16].** That is why if one has no desire for salvation, he or she will never get save. If you have no desire to be filled with the Holy Spirit, God will never fill you with His precious Holy Spirit. He only satisfies the hunger of those who have desire for more of Him. It is based on this principle of desire that Jesus preached His popular sermon on the Mount.

"Blessed are they which do hunger and thirst after righteousness: for they shall be filled" [**Matthew 5:6**].

No matter how powerful a preacher may preach, a bible teacher may teach or a sermon may sound, if his or her audience have no desire for righteousness, they will never surrender their lives to Christ. As an example, there is a gentleman who has been visiting our church for a couple of years now. Whenever I preach and he happens to be in church, he is always one of the first people to

> *God first puts desire into His creation as a drive that will lead them to pursue after its fulfillment and turns around and satisfies that desire in His creation.*

approach me and give his own commentary on the message preached and how good the message is. However, later, I was made to understand that this gentleman has been involving himself in occultic practices, reading occultic materials at home and would not surrender his life to Christ. You can talk to a reluctant person about holiness all you want, they will leave, go home, and forget all about it simply because they have no desire for holiness.

Desire is that which forms the foundation for admittance and acceptance of God's word into ones' heart and life.

Here are a couple of scriptural references that speaks to the principle of desire.

> *"Thou fillest the hungry with good things, and the rich thou hast sent empty away."* **[Luke 1:51]**
>
> *"I will pour water upon him that is thirsty, and floods upon the dry ground".* **[Isaiah 44:3]**

God will always first give His creation a desire and then "He will satisfy the desire of every living thing" according to the bible.

This great principle of desire works in all spheres of ones' life because without desire, there is certainly no drive to get anything accomplished be it spiritual or physical.

The Lord does not give the Holy Spirit to people who are not thirsty for it because He has said in His word that only "*they which do hunger and thirst after righteousness shall be filled*" Therefore the prerequisite for being filled is for one to develop a hunger and thirst for the presence of God in their lives. Based on this principle, instead of constantly praying that Lord will save your children, why don't you rather begin to pray that the Lord will first give them a desire for salvation? ***"God satisfies the* desire *of every living thing" [Psalm 145:16].*** Instead of our churches praying for revival, why don't we begin to pray that God will first give our congregations a desire for his presence.

When you have a burning desire for God's presence, you will cherish that presence and know what to do with it and how to handle it when it comes. On the other hand, if one does not care for God's presence, it's no lost if they do not experience it.

Romans chapter 1; tells us that.

> **_26_For this cause God gave them up unto vile affections: for even their women did change the natural use into that which is against nature: _27_And likewise also the men, leaving the natural use of the woman, burned in their lust one toward another; men with men working that which is unseemly, and receiving in themselves that recompence of their error which was meet.**
>
> **_28_And even as they did not like to retain God in their knowledge, God gave them over to a reprobate mind, to do those things which are not convenient;**

I use to think that this passage of scripture was referring to unbelievers, but I later came to understand that it was actually in reference to believers, people who had already encountered God and had some level of relationship with Him. It reads' ***"when they knew God**, they did not retain Him in their knowledge"* . Meaning, there was certain level of knowledge and acceptance of God, but they drifted away from it by not retaining the knowledge they had received.

Because the people left the natural use of things and

desired to pursue after the un-natural use, God fulfilled that desire and gave them up to their reprobate minds to do those things which are not convenient. Notice that although this example is in the negative sense, but the principle of desire works across the board, whether it has to do with something negative or positive.

This same principle applied to the Jews of bible times. It says in the Scriptures that Pilate gave the Jews the one whom they desired. The Apostle Paul also said; *"You desired a murderer, rather than the Prince of Life"* **[Acts 3:14].** While this may seem like an awful thing to desire, that is in fact what they desired for, and God fulfilled their desire. So, while they got the murderer they desired for, in the person of Barabbas, it's worth noting that they also got murder as a result. The history of the Jewish people through the ages will tell you that no people upon the surface of the earth have been murdered and suffered atrocities continually than the Jews. The holocaust of the Jewish people by Nazi Germany and other acts of antisemitism perpetuated against the Jews goes to prove this point. They chose a murderer in the person of Barabbas over Jesus Christ the sinless lamb of God and the savior of the world and as a result, God gave them up to their desires.

Matt 27;25

- *"24) When Pilate saw that rather a tumult was made, he took water, and washed his hands before the multitude, saying, I am innocent of the blood of this just person; see Ye to it*

- **25) then answered all the people, and said, <u>His blood be on us; and upon our children (descendants)</u>**

Notice from the verse 24 of the scripture above that as Pilate who is not a Jew and who most likely did not have the level of understanding of blood covenant, washed his hand off the innocent blood of Jesus. The Jews on the other hand who are the people of blood covenants and who should have known better rather insisted that the innocent blood of Jesus should be upon them and upon their descendants.

How blind could they be for not seeing the implications of their demands and for calling for the innocent blood of the sinless lamb of God to be upon them and upon their children. In my opinion, the worst thing that the Jews did during the crucifixion of Jesus Christ was not the nail that was driven into his hands. It was not the plated crown of thorns that was forced over his head. It was not the nails that were driven through his feet, nor the whip that tore his back and flesh. It was not even the spear that was driven through his side. The worse thing they did was in the words they spoke over their lives and over that of their descendants coupled with the fact that they were willing to bear the consequences of those words knowingly or unknowingly.

Even Pilate; being a Roman Governor who did not understand the intricacies surrounding blood and blood sacrifices, seem to understand the consequences of shedding innocent blood, and as a result he withdrew himself from the guilt associated with shedding innocent blood, and you mean to tell me that the children of Israel;

the ones whom the Lord had given so many volumes of instructions, ordinances, laws and sacrificial rituals about blood, failed to understand what it means to shed innocent blood? I do not believe that in a minute. They knew what they were doing, and they understood what it was all about but, out of hardness of their hearts they went ahead and had the King of glory to be crucified. That's just like some believers of today. You know what you are doing, and you understand the consequences of the 'double-life' you are living in and out of church, and how it would end you up in hell one day if your ways are not amended, yet the hardness of heart is keeping you from turning around and yielding your life to God. Don't forget that there is an eternal, never ending consequences to the actions we adamantly take even when we know better. It would have been better for them if it was a guilty blood they were tampering with. They touched an innocent blood and on top of that; they ignorantly but boldly took upon themselves and upon their descendants the judgement that comes with the cry of an innocent blood for justice. One thing you can count on God for is that He is always ready to avenge the cry of an innocent blood.

Since then, look at what the descendants of these Jewish people had suffered through the ages and have still been going through as a nation. In the history of humanity; no race, nor people of any color or descent had been through some of the horrific past of the Jewish people. Even today, there exist museums around the world (Holocaust Museum) built just to commemorate the degree of suffering of the Jewish people. No other people, race, ethnicity upon the surface of this earth had ever experienced what they had gone through and are still going through in the Middle East and other parts of the world which has Jewish populations.

I believe with my whole heart, and I am of the conviction that it's all because of the consequences of the innocent blood they pronounced upon not only themselves but also upon their descendants. I submit to you that all the antisemitic crimes and atrocities committed against Jewish people even until today; may have its roots in the judgement in relation to the 'innocent blood' they took upon themselves and their descendants.

"Let His blood be on us; and upon our children (descendants)".

Because according to the book of Lamentations, when the fathers' sin and they are no more, the consequences of those sins are visited upon their children and children's children. King Solomon; in all his wisdom; in naming the seven things God hate the most, saw it fit to add to the list "hands that shed innocent blood". **Proverbs 6;16–19**

These six things doth the Lord the; yea seven are an abomination unto Him.

1. *a proud look*
2. *A lying tongue*
3. ***Hands that shed innocent blood***
4. *A Heart that devises wicked plot*
5. *A feet that is swift in running to mischief*
6. *A false witness that speakers lies*
7. *He that soweth discord among brethren*

Again, in their wilderness travels with Moses as their leader, they desired flesh and they said to God, ***"Our*** *soul loatheth this light bread that comes down from heaven* **[Numbers 21:5],** *angels' food* **[Psalm 78:25]. *"We remember the fleshpots of Egypt"* [Exodus 16:3].** And the Bible says that they received what they desired for, but it came with leanness in their souls **[Psalm 106:15].**

The lesson here is that if you keep pressing God against His will, He will give you up to your desires, but the downside will be that it will come with leanness in your soul. That is exactly what happened to Balaam when he persistently went to God for permission to curse the Jews because of the personal gains that was promised to him by Balaak. Like King David said, what you rather ought to do is to ask God to cleanse your desire and create in you a clean and pure heart and desire. As a parent, the best prayer you can pray for a sons or daughters who has gone astray from the Lord is to pray that God create in them a *desire* for righteousness and salvation, or a desire to be drawn to God because God will not act against their will if they have no desire for Him. So here the Scripture says that *"Thou visitest the earth with water when thou hast made it to desire it"* [verse 9, KJV]. The earth desires rain, but it is God who puts that desire in the earth. He satisfies the longing soul. That is how the free will that God gave mankind works.

One must understand that as human beings, our will controls our destiny. One must also understand that the will of man is one of the most precious gifts God gave us, but also one of the most dangerous.

That makes it a very dangerous component of our being as humans. Acting in accordance or against the will of God is totally the choice of humans because God gave us the freedom to exercise our will, but this can also lead to detrimental consequence if our will is not exercise within the confines of the will of God for our lives.

Let me draw your attention to a verse in Joel:

23. *Be glad then, ye children of Zion, and rejoice in the LORD your God: for he hath given you the former rain moderately, and he will cause to come down for you the rain, the former rain, and the latter rain in the first month.*

24. *And the floors shall be full of wheat, and the vats shall overflow with wine and oil.*

25. *And I will restore to you the years that the locust hath eaten, the cankerworm, and the caterpillar, and the palmerworm, my great army which I sent among you.*

> *Our will is precious because, God gave you the same power of the will that He possess. Also, our human 'will' is dangerous because it gives you the ability to choose against the will of the one who gave us the will.*

> **26. And ye shall eat in plenty, and be satisfied, and praise the name of the LORD your God, that hath dealt wondrously with you: and my people shall never be ashamed.**
>
> **27. And ye shall know that I am in the midst of Israel, and that I am the LORD your God, and none else: and my people shall never be ashamed.**
> **Joel 2:23-27**

Now let's look at a further reference from the Epistle of James. James is speaking about patience, and farming, and he says:

> **Be patient therefore, brethren, unto the coming of the Lord. Behold, the husbandman waiteth for the precious fruit of the earth, and hath long patience for it, until he receives the early and latter rain.**
> **James 5:7**

According to Joel's prophesy, God has *"… given you the former rain moderately,"* that is, in due season, *"and He will cause to come down for you the rain, the former rain and the latter rain, in the first month"* **Joel 2:23.**

What's your Focus: watching for the Antichrist or Being Like Christ?

Now, there are many different opinions about revival. There are those who preach that there can be no revival before Jesus comes. They say that conditions are such that no revival can happen. They are so certain that they have the right interpretation of prophecy because they have worked it out very cleverly. They say that what we should be looking for in our day and age is the antichrist and not revival.

The only scriptures I know on this subject keep us looking for Christ and not for an Anti-Christ. I strongly deprecate the sort of prophecy-mongering that keeps our eyes constantly looking for an antichrist. The subtle design of Satan in all this is to get people far more concerned about prophecy than about being like Jesus. Now the Holy Spirit doesn't draw us to the contemplation of prophecy. The Holy Spirit draws us to the contemplation of prophecy only to remind us that of the day and the hour of the Lord's coming, none of us know, so we had better be ready when He does come. What the Holy Ghost does impress upon us concerning prophecy is that we should be ready! Watch therefore!

The three last parables of Jesus were on this very subject. The three last parables that Jesus ever gave to His disciples, before He went to the cross, were:

1. *"The Parable of the Ten Virgins"* **[Matthew 25:1-10]**;
2. *"The Parable of the Talents"* **[verses 14–30];** *and*
3. *"The Parable of the Judgment of the Nations"* **[verses 31-46].**

The first parable, the one about the ten virgins, is given for the church to be watchful. ***"Watch, therefore, for ye know not the hour nor the day of His coming"* [verse 13].**

The point of the second parable, the one concerning the talents, is for the believer and the church to be faithful in what God gives us to do. The third parable, the one about the Judgment of the Nations, where they are judged

> *The Holy Spirit is deeply interested in you knowing something about prophecy, but only in order that you should be faithful, watchful, and be merciful; for these are the three tests of a genuine Christian.*

according as to how they have dealt with "little ones," and whether they have taken care of the little ones and the weary ones, and the stricken ones, and the ones that had no food and clothes, and the ones that were sick, and the ones that were in prison—it is according to how they have dealt with those that they have judged. This is the word of the Lord for us to be merciful.

The key here is not whether you know who the antichrist is nor when he shall be revealed because that is totally irrelevant to your spiritual growth and wellbeing as a believer.

CHAPTER 3

THE FORMER (EARLY) RAINS

The phrase the "former and latter" rains occurs multiple times in the Bible and the exact wording varies from version to version. Among credible biblical examples of this phrase in both the Old and the New Testaments are; *Deuteronomy 11:14; Jeremiah 5:24; Hosea 6:3; Joel 2:23; Zechariah 10:1 and James 5:7*

There are at least two different meanings given to the expression "latter and former rain" which is also translated as "early and late rain,". It can also be translated as the "first rain and the latter rain" or "autumn and spring rains." In Israel the early rains came in the autumn (October-November) and the latter rain came in the spring (March-April).

One interpretation assumes a literal meaning and the other a spiritual meaning of the expression. Literally as in Deuteronomy 11:13-15 is part of a promise that God gave to the nation of Israel that if they would love Him (Deuteronomy 11:1) and keep His commandments (Deuteronomy 11:8) then He would bless them. The blessing is described in the entire chapter and verses 13-15 is a promise of enough rain to grow their crops and feed their animals.

> *"It shall come about, if you listen obediently to my commandments which I am commanding you today, to love the LORD your God and to serve Him with all your heart and all your soul, that He will give the rain for your land in its season, the early and late rain, that you may gather in your grain and your new wine and your oil. He will give grass in your fields for your cattle, and you will eat and be satisfied."*
> **Deuteronomy 11:13-15 (NASB)**

God is not a dead God nor is He the God of dead things. He is the God of all life because all things whatsoever exist, emanated from Him. Hence God by His nature, love to revive His creation and this includes humanity whom like no other creation, was created in the image of God. John 10:10 declares that *"I am come that they might have life, and have it more abundantly"*

Joel's declaration that; *"He has given you the former rain moderately and He will give you the latter rain abundantly"* **Joel 2:23** fits perfectly into the nature of God and the conception that God will revive His people.

> *"Come and let us return unto the Lord, for he has smitten and He will heal, he has torn and he will bind together…"*
> **Hosea 6:1-2**

In this part of the world, (North America and Canada) we don't have former and latter rains. Hence to better understand how the former and latter rains occur naturally, the Psalmist description given in Psalm 65 will be of a great help in characterizing the two rainy seasons in the land of Palestine.

Psalm 65:9-13 (KJV)

> ***Thou visitest the earth, and waterest it: thou greatly enrichest it with the river of God, which is full of water: thou preparest them corn, when thou hast so provided for it. [10] Thou waterest the ridges thereof abundantly: thou settlest the furrows thereof: thou makest it soft with showers: thou blessest the springing thereof. [11] Thou crownest the year with thy goodness; and thy paths drop fatness. [12] They drop upon the pastures of the wilderness: and the little hills rejoice on every side. [13] The pastures are clothed with flocks; the valleys also are covered over with corn; they shout for joy, they also sing.***

However, the caution one must exercise here is that the reason why God says He will give you the former rain "moderately" is because "If the farmer has continual rain, he looks with despair upon his wheat fields, knowing that the continual rain will wash away the seeds sown and also make stalk of those seeds that manage to grow so thin, so mushy, so green, and will end up eventually falling over.

MODERATION

Hence, God in his infinite wisdom promises that; *"I will give you the former rains 'moderately'*

The first question that comes to mind is that, why is it that the former rains must be given in moderate proportions as compared to the latter rains that God promises to give abundantly. Is it because God cannot supply in full capacity the former rain as He does the latter? Or it is because God has a plan for supplying the former rains in moderate proportions only?

Meanings of 'Moderation' according to Dictionary. com are;

i.   *Keeping within reasonable or proper limits.*
ii. *Means – not extreme, excessive, or intense.*
iii. *It means, just the 'fair' amount needed at a particular point in time due to a particular reason.*

God in his infinite wisdom, have decided to give the former rains moderately because of the purpose for which the former rain serves. The former rain is given by God to soften the hard clods of soil that have been made so hard through the long dry period, and God softens them with the former rain in preparation for the sowing of seed. The seed is sown at that period. That's why the former rain ought to be given moderately so as not to wash away the seed that has been sown. So, God, by the former rain, and by the moisture in the earth, springs the corn. With much more rain than it will need, the stalk may look strong and big in appearance, but its thin, green, and fresh and would have no strength in it, such that the slightest wind may cause it to bend and drop and the farmers' hope of a good harvest would be eventually lost. Hence the reason for a moderate former rain.

This is just like any other of God's blessings that He bestows upon his children. He first blesses us in moderate proportions to test our faithfulness before He bestows abundant blessings. If one is not faithful in little, God will

> *God will not trust you with a flock if He can not trust you with a lamb.*

hardly add more to the little that one has. That is why it calls on every child of God to be faithful in the handling of the initial small blessings that God brings into our lives. Remember what Jesus told Peter about his flock before He departed away from them? He said to Peter to feed his lamb before he asked him to feed His flock.

The implication here is that if one cannot be faithful with a single lamb, then feeding a flock will be too overwhelming and almost impossible for them to handle because they would not be faithful with the greater demands that comes with increased responsibilities either.

CHAPTER 4

PERIOD OF DRYNESS

After the former rains has been given moderately, then comes Gods dry spell or the dry season which hardens the wheat stalk and makes them strong in preparation towards bearing and supporting the ears of wheat. This period of dryness is an interlude between the former rains that comes upon the land first and the latter rains that follows on later in the agricultural season in the land of Palestine.

When the bible speaks of 'corn', don't be thinking about the Indian corn or other types that we have become accustomed to in our part of the world because it's not referring to 'corn' as we know it. In fact, the Jewish tradition knows nothing about Indian corn (maize) that we use today. Every reference to corn in the Old Testament means 'wheat' or barley, because that was what was grown by the Jews in the land of Palestine in those days. That was their staple crop hence 'corn' was just used as a generic term to describe grains in general. So now the early showers known as the former or early rains spring the corn (wheat) and the corn then begins to grow.

The early saturation of the dry patched grounds lasts for a while, but then passes away and cease. Now the corn has been established and its roots have gone down into the soil. What happens next is that the roots begin to draw whatever moisture it can get from the drying soil and from the atmosphere as well. At this time, as the stalk is being formed, the dryness (because the former rains are over) causes the wheat stalk not to be soft, but rather to be hard.

The Wheat Stalk

Upon examination of the typical wheat stalk, you will find that the stalk has 'knots' all up the stem. They are God's wonderful provision to keep the stalk erect because without the knots on the wheat stalk, it would bend over under the weight of the grains and fall to the ground before maturation, hence the wheat grains will be lost.

> *There are periods in our lives when God's will bring dryness to our souls. It is to give us the appetite to desire more of Him.*

The Formation of the knots & the hard stalk

But, how does God make those knots, and how does God make the stalk strong? It is worth noting that the knots are formed, and the stalk is made strong by a dry period. This is the period of dryness between the former rain and latter rains. In between the former and latter rain there is a dry period when God is forming the stalk and making it strong. If the farmer has continual rain, he looks with despair upon his wheat fields, because he knows that the stalk will be so thin, so mushy, so green, that it will fall over as mentioned earlier in the previous chapter.

It may be strong and big in appearance, but since it's thin, it has no strength in it, and the slightest wind will make it bend and drop, causing the farmer's wheat to be lost and the hope of bountiful harvest gone with it.

- *You will go through some time of heartaches*
- *A time when everything that can go wrong will seem to be going wrong in your life.*
- *There are times when it may even seem like the Lord had forsaken you or don't even care about you anymore.*

Jesus being the son of God, yet felt that way at a point in his life as he cried.

> ***"Eli, Eli lama-saba-thani; My LORD; My LORD why hast thou forsaken me".***

But don't be dismay because if Jesus being the Son of God felt that way, then don't be surprised when you do feel the same. Like the corn stalk, it could be a time of neutrality; God has not left you, He is there with you, but it may seem as if you don't feel his presence. God did not leave Jesus; When all the sins of humanity were laid upon him; the Holy God, turned away his face from him but did not leave him.

In **Isaiah 40:27**, when the nation of Israel was going through their period of dryness, they lamented as if to say that God had forgotten them.

> *"Why sayest thou, O Jacob, and speakest thou, O' Israel, My way is hid from the LORD, and my judgment is passed over from my God?"*

The life application here is that; God will often bring you through times of spiritual dryness, which is represented by times of sorrow, pain, discomfort and even disappointments to make you strong. But thank God that He brings you *'through'* and not *'to'*. Bringing you 'to' will mean that's your final destination, but bringing you 'through' means it's a temporal position that will come to pass. In other words, God will make sure that you don't get stuck in your down times and times of pain and sorrow.

The Psalmist puts it all well when he stated in **Psalms 23***:*

> *"...Ye though I walk "through" the valley of the shadow of death, I will fear no evil. For thou art with me..."*

Thank God that in moments of our trials and temptations, He makes us to walk 'through' and not walk 'to'.

The reason why you will not be stuck in 'the valley of the shadow of death' is because even in that fearful valley He restores your soul. He keeps your mind intact and gives you peace through the process so you will not disintegrate and fall apart. This is beside the fact that if you endure these trials of your faith God will soon cause your cup to run over. So, God will often take you *"through"* times of spiritually dryness, sorrow, pain & disappointments to make you strong like the wheat stalk. Its sound paradoxical to say this, but your pain, sorrow and disappointments, and moments of dryness is a sign that God loves you. I know this is hard to swallow and you may be saying to yourself, hello Pastor; am I hearing right? Yes, you are hearing right. Your disappointments are nothing but a sign that the good Lord loves you and watches over you.

> *"For whom the Lord loveth, He chasteneth, and scourgeth every son whom he receiveth."* **Hebrews 12:6**

Listen to me friend; there are some prosperity preachers out there who will want to make you believe that the Lord will give you joy, joy, joy, all day, and every day. And if that's not the case then it means something is wrong with your spiritual life, but that's just not true of the child of God. I totally denounce and dismiss that notion because like the wheat stalk; God will often bring you through a period of dryness in your life to make you strong and well prepared for the latter rains that He is going to pour upon you abundantly. A weak and feeble stalk cannot survive the latter rains because those rains unlike the former rain, pours abundantly. Like the wheat stalk, much glory in your soul, many happy occasions, much clapping of hands, and joy, joy, joy in the Lord alone will not make you strong.

Your pain, sorrows, and chastisement are the dry and hard stalk. When the joy is mixed with chastisement, it will make you strong, and that's why the Lord brings you through it. He doesn't bring you through to abandoned you; rather, it's a sign that he loves and cares for you. That's what God does in nature to the stalk of plants around us. If God in His infinite wisdom will do that to a mere plant in order for the plant to become strong in

> *Too much of the former rain than you really need will rather make your spiritual stalk weak instead of growing you to be strong in the Lord and in your walk with God.*

later season of its life, then He will even more so do it to us seeing that we are part of nature and of his creation whom he loves more than the plant. That is why God did not create other animals or plants in his image, but He did create you in his image and likeness, and that alone makes you a special breed among all of God's creation. Believe it or not - you are.

CHAPTER 5

THE LATTER RAINS

After the former rains, comes the dry spell and after the dry spell comes the *Latter Rains.* The latter rains in the land of Palestine, comes somewhere around the month of April, and this precede the Great Harvest which is to come afterwards.

Understand that the reason why the latter rain is very important is because, after the former rains and the dry season had occurred; everything that happens next into the harvest depends on the magnitude of the latter rain. The purpose of the former rains and the dry season is to prepare the land, the seed, and the wheat stalk. However, the advent of the latter rains is crucial because it is the latter rains that determines how great the harvest is going to be for a particular farming season. A farmer can have a good amount of former rain as needed and good dry season that strengthens the stalk, but without a successful latter rain, all hope of a good harvest will be lost.

For short, the latter rain signify revival itself, and the harvest that comes after the latter rain, is the product of that revival. And so, notice that unlike the former rain that God promises to give only in moderate proportions, God on the other hand sends the latter rain *'abundantly'* in order that there may be an *'abundant'* harvest. This is because in the land of Palestine it is the abundant latter rain that plumps the ears of corn or wheat and leads to full ears of wheat after which God in His infinite wisdom, sends the sunshine to ripen the wheat grains.

God is a God of revival as well as a God of life. He loves to revive His people and His creation in general since he is not a dead God. Just as God promises the latter rains in abundance, he also promises life in abundance in the form of eternal life through Jesus Christ.

> *"I am come that they might have life and might have it more abundantly"* **[John 10:10].**

This passage of Scripture

> *"He has given you the former rain moderately and He will give you the latter rain abundantly"* **[Joel 2:23]**

really fits in with the conception that God will revive His people. Now what is the "former and latter rain"? In this part of the world, we don't have former and latter rain. But in Palestine where this word was written, they have very definite signs and times of rain. What David mentions in Psalm 65 is really describing the former and the latter rains. So, Psalm 65, characterizes the former rain. In Psalm 65; notice that the first portion; verses 9-10, speaks of the former rains, when it says.

> *"Thou visitest the earth. Thou waterest the ridges thereof. Thou makest it soft with showers".*

This declaration by the Psalmist is describing the intent of the former rains. But then the verse 11, begins to tell us about the *"latter rains"* when it says.

> *"Thou crownest the year with Thy goodness"*

That is the latter rain because whatever God began from the former rain, He also crowns it with His goodness which represent abundant harvest. When you read further to the verses 12-13 of the same chapter, something interesting also happens.

> *"They drop upon the pastures of the wilderness; and the little hills rejoice on every side. The pastures are clothed with flocks; the valleys also are covered over with corn; they shout for joy, they also sing."*
>
> *".......... they shout for joy, they also sing."*

What does this mean? If you have ever witnessed a field of wheat, especially when the wind blows through on a windy day, it really 'sings' or make a unique sound.

At least that is the term used by farmers to describe the sound made by the fields of wheat or corn. So as the wind passes over the wheat field, all the heads bow in unison and in one accord, they begin to 'sing' by the sound they make as the wind is passes through. But notice that the singing of the wheat will only occur when it is in good full ear. In other words, the fields of wheat doesn't sing when the ear isn't formed. And so again, latter rain is very important because it is that which plumps the ears of wheat and leads to the '*bowing and singing*' of the heads of wheat.

It signifies the outpouring of the Holy Spirit upon God's people because the "bowing and singing" is created by the medium of a wind and wind in the bible symbolizes the breath of God and the move of the Holy Spirit. The reason why it typifies the outpouring of the Holy Spirit upon Gods people is because; *Wind*; in Hebrew "*Ruwah*", *also* means *breath or Spirit.*

That's why in the book of creations (Genesis) it is written that; **Genesis 1-2;** after the creation of the Heaven and the Earth; ***"Spirit of God had to move; in order for things to come to life"***

And so, it is the *'bowing and the singing'* created by the wind of God that brings us revival and life. That's why the Prophet Hosea; in speaking about the end time revival in Hosea 6:1-3, referred to the outpouring of the former and latter rains together. The implication here is that the outpouring of the former and Latter rain is the recipe needed for true revival.

A Word of Prophecy

The Disappearance of the former and latter rains:

After the time of Jesus, however, there was terrible depredations in the land of Palestine. After Jerusalem was destroyed by the Romans, the temple was destroyed as well, and many Jews were taken into captivity in Babylon.

As a result of these captivities leading to the cutting down of trees by the armies of the aliens who conquered Jerusalem, the land of Palestine plunged into awful, dry period for many centuries. Because the people were taken away into captivity, agriculture practically ceased and the tress did not sprout hence Palestine plunged into deforestation, leading to the disappearance of the "former and latter rains". So, for centuries, the former and latter rains ceased and totally disappeared, and the land of Palestine became almost barren.

Restoration of the Former and Latter Rains.

In a biblical sense this represented the period in the history of Israel when God forsook Israel; and although it lasted for centuries, this would not last forever because God referred to this period as being forsaken for a 'little while'.

God spoke through the Prophet Isaiah saying.
Isaiah 54;7-8

"For a small moment have I forsaken thee; but with great mercies will I gather

49

> *thee. In a little wrath I hid my face from thee for a moment; but with everlasting kindness will I have mercy on thee, saith the Lord thy Redeemer."*

This brief period of God's abandonment of Israel was revealed not only to the Prophet Isaiah but also to Zechariah in Zechariah 1:16 and to a few other prophets of God.

Zechariah 1:16 (KJV)

> *Therefore, thus saith the Lord; I am returned to Jerusalem with mercies: my house shall be built in it, saith the Lord of hosts, and a line shall be stretched forth upon Jerusalem.*

Hosea 6:1–3 says.

> *"Come and let us return unto the Lord: for he hath torn, and he will heal us; he hath smitten, and he will bind us up. [2] After two days will he revive us: in the third day he will raise us up, and we shall live in his sight. [3] Then shall we know, if we follow on to know the Lord: his going forth is prepared as the morning; and he shall come unto us as the rain, as the latter and former rain unto the earth"*

History therefore reveals to us that God worked His miracle and after the first world war, God opened

Palestine for Israel and Jews all over the world began to return home to the land of Palestine which eventually culminated in the coming together of the modern-day Jewish nation in 1948.

Modern history also tells us that the Jewish people came from Russia, Azerbaijan, (former USSR), parts of Europe, (especially Easter Europe), Ethiopia, Asia and from all around the globe where they were scattered and headed towards what centuries ago used to be homeland to their forefathers.

Isaiah 54;7 *"For a small moment have I forsaken thee; but with great mercies will I gather thee.*

Do you not see a spiritual significance in this? – that as the Lord gathers His people the Jews from all around the world, it is an indication that the coming of the Lord draweth nigh?

The Reason for the return of the Jews to the Homeland.

> *The big picture pertaining to the return of the Jews to their homeland is so God will bring back the former and the latter rains to the land of Palestine that has long suffered from drought and deforestation.*

Furthermore, the reason for bringing back the former and the latter rains is so the ears of wheat will be able to "bow into singing" which again signifies for the New Testament church, an outpouring by the wind of God (Holy Spirit) leading to a revival upon God's people. So, for hundreds of years, these rains ceased, but then the Jews began to go back home and after they had repopulated the land of Palestine and planted forest all over the land of Palestine, the *former rains* began to come back to the land.

Latter Rain is back as well

But the wonder of wonders is that; as the restoration and reforestation continued; another wonderful thing happened, which is the latter rains also came back in addition to the return of the former rains. There was a publication recently in the *"Herald of His Coming"* by a news Correspondent in Palestine announcing the truth that "The Latter rains had begun to fall again in Israel".

So, in Palestine at the present, the old former and latter rains that used to be but ceased and disappear for several hundreds of years; has come back again.

And so, God has fulfilled His word; in that

i) *Israel is back together as a nation.*
ii) *God has restored the 'former rains'*
iii) *And now, God has brought back the latter rains as well.*

That is a wonderful fulfillment of prophesy in **Joel 2:23** *"I have given you the former rain moderately, I will give you the latter rain abundantly"*

Awake Church; Awake people of God.!

When all these things are happening, – Do you still not see a spiritual significance in this; that the coming of the Lord draweth nigh. Matthew's gospel declared that: *'when ye shall see all these things happen, it's time to look up; for thy redemption dessert nigh even the salvation of your soul''*

God is desiring to see again– the heads of wheat 'bow and burst out into singing? The Prophet Isaiah captured this in **Isaiah 54:**1 when he prophesied and said.

> *"Sing, O barren, thou that didst not bear; break forth into singing, and cry loud, thou that didst not travail; for more are the children of the desolate than the children of the married wife saith the LORD"*

i)   *The Jews after many centuries in captivity have returned home to the land of Palestine.*

ii) *God has restored the 'Former Rains'*

iii) *And now, he has brought back the Latter rains as well.*

And so as there first come the *former rains;* then also comes a *dry season.* After the dry season, comes the *latter rain;* and after the later rain comes the bowing and singing of the fields of wheat; which represent the great outpouring by the wind of God and after that comes what I would like to discuss in the next chapter, which has to do with the final Great harvest, the sound of abundant of rain. These are signs of a resounding Apostolic awakening and revival in this end times. Jesus is coming soon. Sooner than you ever think. Are you prepared to meet Him when He comes?

CHAPTER 6

THE GREAT HARVEST

> *The key to bible prophesy is not "This is going to be that". That would be a mere mental calculations and speculation.*

The key to bible prophesy is not *"This is going to be that".* That would be a mere mental calculations and speculation. Rather and according to the Apostle Peter on the day of Pentecost; God's key to biblical prophecy is *"This is that"* as declared by Peter. This is because the phrase 'this is that' speaks to something being precise and not a mere speculation. This tells of the mind of the Spirit which is also precise because the bible declares in **I Timothy 4:1-2** that the Spirit speaketh expressly

> *"1 Now the Spirit speaketh expressly, that in the latter times some shall depart from the faith, giving heed to seducing spirits, and doctrines of devils;*
>
> *2 Speaking lies in hypocrisy; having their conscience seared with a hot iron"*

The Amplified version of the bible puts it this way.

> *"But the [Holy] Spirit distinctly and expressly declares that in latter times some will turn away from the faith, giving attention to deluding and seducing spirits and doctrines that demons teach,"*

The word '*expressly*' means **to be outspoken and distinctly clear not by mere hint, and symbols, and shadowy images of the future, but rather in an open and plain manner**. This implies the Spirit of the Lord makes utterance with no shadow of doubt nor gray areas.

Although God does not tell you what is going to happen in every detail to fulfill prophesies, what God does reveal to his people in the fulfillment of prophesy when it takes place is expressly clear because it is the voice of the Spirit. That is true all the way through the pages of scripture from the book of Genesis to the book of Revelation.

Examples 1. *In the book of Acts (Acts 2:16)* Peter by the leading of the Spirit said in reference to Joel's prophesy*; "This is that" which was spoken by the Prophet Joel*......

Example 2.

When the devout man Simon and the 84 years old

prophetess Anna came into the temple and saw the baby Jesus; (Luke 2:25-38), they by the leading of the Spirit knew *"This is that"* which God has promised and as a result, they announced "This is the Messiah". From this, one can see again that bible prophecy is not speculation as we have seen some people do when they hear something about you or know something about somebody and yet claim its coming from God.

Example 3. When the 70 years period of Israel being in exile had reached, Daniel knew exactly by the Spirit (not by calculation nor speculation) that the 70 years prophesied was up and that Israel must begin to go back to the land of Palestine. And so, Daniel started to pray and to seek God's face and it was through Daniel's prayer and intercession that Nehemiah and Ezra went back to the Holy land to rebuild the walls of Jerusalem and to begin to restore temple worship. The same applies to Zechariah when he saw the vision among the myrtle tree on the 70th year of the exile.

Based on these and other examples in the bible; we can truthfully say that God has fulfilled His word because the latter rains, just like the former rains, are coming down today in the land of Israel after many centuries of its absence. Since the former rains and the latter rains has both returned after many centuries of its absence, it is an indication that we are close to the time when the Son of Man shall come back and reap His harvest.

The Former rains are back
The Latter rains are back
And obviously what is next in line is the 'Great Harvest'.

I believe that God is going to give us an abundant, glory showers of the latter rain before the return of the Lord Jesus Christ to reap the church home to glory. This is what Haggai saw in Haggai 2:9 (KJV) when he said.

> *"The glory of this latter house shall be greater than of the former, saith the Lord of hosts: ……"*

The bible says Christ is coming for a glorious church not a defeated church nor a feeble church so, there must be a great outpouring of the latter rain for the harvest to be glorious. According to the book of Revelation, the harvest of souls must be *"a great multitude, which no man can number"* I'm not making this up; and if you think I'm making this up check for yourself what Revelation 7;9 says.

Revelation 7:9 (KJV)

> *"After this I beheld, and, lo, a great multitude, which no man could number, of all nations, and kindreds, and people, and tongues, stood before the throne, and before the Lamb, clothed with white robes, and palms in their hands;"*

Don't' even waste your time thinking about how God is going to do it because like Elijah; just when you think you are the only one left standing for God; that's when God is going to show you that there are 5000 and more others of his servants who have not yet bow to Baal worship nor to the systems of this world. Just stand firm and don't be discourage because you are not alone. Some time ago, I had a conversation with a Ghanaian Pastor based in Japan and he was telling me of how in Japan, a country that is dominated by Buddhism; how thousands are coming to accept the Lord, baptized in the name of Jesus, and filled with the Holy Ghost and fire. All these things are happening not in only Japan but also in many parts of the world in preparation for the great harvest of souls before the coming of the Lord. Not to name several testimonies from other parts of the world including communist stronghold nations of China, Russia and more.

THE GREAT HARVEST

It is a matter of common knowledge that the harvest is always the culmination of all the efforts that farmers put into their work. After the earth has opened its mouth due to dryness and desired rain from the Lord, the former and latter rains are the fulfillment of this desire. The product of these rains is the harvest of crops.

> *For lack of clarity, the harvest has often been perceived as one big event however, there are three distinct parts to the great harvest.*

Notice that the harvest of old in the land of Palestine; comprised of 3 major parts.

1. *The Harvest of the First fruit*
2. *The General Harvest*
3. *The Final Reaping.*

Each of these phases of harvest has a spiritual implication and significance in God's timetable of events of the end time. I will expound on each of these harvests to bring clarity.

1. THE HARVEST OF THE FIRST FRUITS

Revelation 14; gives a description of the harvest of the first fruits. This is the first phase of the great harvest. Notice that this is distinct and serve a different purpose from the general harvest and the final reaping aspect of the great harvest.

Revelation 14:1-4 (KJV)

"And I looked, and, lo, a Lamb stood on the mount Sion, and with him a hundred forty and four thousand, having his father's name written in their foreheads. [2] And I heard a voice from heaven, as the voice of many waters, and as the voice of a great thunder: and I heard the voice of harpers harping with their harps: [3] And they sung as it were a new song before the throne, and before the four beasts, and the elders: and no man could

> *learn that song but the hundred and forty and four thousand, which were redeemed from the earth. [4] These are they which were not defiled with women; for they are virgins. These are they which follow the Lamb whithersoever he goeth. These were redeemed from among men, <u>being the first fruits unto God and to the Lamb.</u>*

This is where many religious groups and denominations, including the Jehovah Witnesses have erred by claiming that only a hundred forty and four thousand people are going to be candidates of heaven. However, if you read a little further into the text, in Rev. 14: you will find out that the hundred forty and four thousand mentioned in this passage refers only to the first fruit of the total harvest and not the entire harvest of souls. Revelations 14:4; speaks only about a minute portion of the Great harvest of souls that's known as **"the first fruits unto God and the lamb".**

In principle, Israel was not allowed to reap their harvest until they had first offered unto God the 'first fruits'. Now, the first fruit is only a very small part of the entire harvest. It is far smaller compared to the rest of the harvest. The significance of the first fruits in the land of Israel is that; It acknowledges that God is the owner and provider of all the blessings that they will be reaping from the harvest. In today's term, the first fruits are like acknowledging that God owns your car, your house, your job, your income and even your livelihood since all blessings comes from above and from the father of all who is also above all as well as the giver of all good gifts. This is because it is God who has favored us and who blesses us with all good things. Notice I said 'things' because that's how the bible usually refers to material stuff. What some people sell their eternal souls for are nothing but just 'things'.

That is why the bible says, ***"Seek ye first the kingdom of God and its righteousness and all other things shall be added unto you"***

Furthermore, in speaking about material things another scripture says *"these things do the pagans go after"*. Our prime motive for serving the Lord should not be to accumulate 'things' or to be simply blessed with 'material stuff'. It should be about pursuing for his righteousness, peace, and justice. All other purposes should be secondary. The nation of Israel could only reap their harvest, after they had offered that first fruit- that which was their best and first harvest unto God.

Another significance of the first fruit is that God takes what you have offered in reverence to Him, and He intend blesses the remaining lump from which you gave the first fruit. So, at the end, you happen to be the winner. I can share the testimonies of some members of our church who trusted God enough to give a first fruit offering of their income to God, and the testimonies that comes out of those faithful and sacrificial giving each year are phenomenal. Some who are landlords had a whole year rent paid to them on the spot by their tenants. Some had their income doubled by their employers for no apparent reason. Some at least two brethren had the ownership of real estate property turned over into their names by deceased relatives. Listen to me brothers and sisters – things like that don't happen by chance or by magic, because I have seen people die and they are so selfish even in death that they prefer for the State to take over their estate than to turn it over as a legacy to any relative or people they know who are close to them.

2) THE GENERAL HARVEST

After the harvest of the first fruits, comes the '*general harvest*'.

Revelations 14:6 *"Then I saw another angel fly in the midst of heaven, having the everlasting gospel to preach unto them that dwell on the earth, and to every nation, and kindred, and tongue, and people"*

Notice that this is not to a 144,000 people because the 144,000 was only the first fruit. Notice what the verse is saying here, "having the everlasting gospel." There is only one gospel which is the everlasting gospel. So, the bible says in **Galatians 1:8 (KJV)**

> ***"But though we, or an angel from heaven, preach any other gospel unto you than that which we have preached unto you, let him be accursed."***

And then when you go on to the verse 14 (Rev. 14:14), The Lord Himself emerge and begins to reap His own people and that represents the 'General Harvest' of souls.

Revelation 14:14-16 (KJV)

> *And I looked, and behold a white cloud, and upon the cloud one sat like unto the Son of man, (Jesus) having on his head a golden crown, and in his hand a sharp sickle.*
>
> *[15] And another angel came out of the temple, crying with a loud voice to him that sat on the cloud, thrust in thy sickle, and reap for the time is come for thee to reap; for the harvest of the earth is ripe.*
>
> *16] And he that sat on the cloud (Jesus) thrust in his sickle on the earth; and the earth was reaped.*

These texts do not refer to the harvest of the first fruits because of the magnitude of the harvest. Neither does it refer to the final reaping because that will be done by angels according to scripture. These texts are all in reference to the general harvest of souls that will occur on the day of the rapture.

3) THE FINAL REAPING

After the harvest of the '*first fruit*' and the '*general harvest*', comes the third and final segment of the harvest known as the "Final Reaping". So back to our text in Revelation 14: then finally comes another reaping (Rev. 14: 17-20)

Revelation 14:17-20 (KJV)

"And another angel came out of the temple, which is in heaven, he also having a sharp sickle. [18] And another angel came out from the altar, which had power over fire; and cried with a loud cry to him that had the sharp sickle, saying, thrust in thy sharp sickle, and gather the clusters of the vine of the earth;(that's the 3rd and final harvest) for her grapes are fully ripe. [19] And the angel thrust in his sickle into the earth, and gathered the vine of the earth, and cast it into the great winepress of the wrath of God. [20] And the winepress was trodden without the city, and blood came out of the winepress, even unto the horse bridles, by the space of a thousand and six hundred furlongs."

Now Notice the following.

1) whilst the general harvest was done by Christ Himself; the final reaping on the other hand was executed by an angel.
2) whilst in the harvest of the first fruits and the general harvest, God gathered or reaped His own people, - in the 'final reaping' that was not the case.

Therefore, let's see what happens in the final reaping; The first angel thrust in his sickle to the earth (verse

19) but it's interesting what he gathers this time around. Notice that he gathers not the corn, and not the wheat, which would have represented the actual harvest – which is God's own people but rather the angel gathers the vine. And let's see what the angel did with the vine? – He cast it into the winepress of the wrath of God and blood comes out.

The third and last segment of the great harvest therefore is the final judgement of the wicked.

That's The Grapes of Wrath
That's the final reaping
That's the doom of the wicked.

Listen Friend; The time of reaping of the Lord Jesus is coming soon. If you are not reaped among the first fruits; and you are not reaped among the general harvest by the Lord Jesus Christ Himself; then it means your only option will be to be reaped not as part of the real harvest of God's own people, but rather as a vine during the final reaping. And you should know by now where the harvest of the vine goes; the verse says it goes to eternal damnation with the wicked. I therefore announce to you with fear and trembling that; *" These are the days of the last showers of the latter rains"* You better get in now or be left behind eternally, because there is no middle grounds when it comes to eternal destinations. It is either one makes it to heaven or die and go to hell, but the choice is absolutely yours to make.

CHAPTER 7

THE REVIVAL

I like those words that usually begin with 're' because for most part, they are the type of words that brings back hope into hopeless situations. They are usually the kind of words that tells us to go back to how things use to be or how things are supposed to be.

So, I looked in the strong concordance for words that align with the word 'revival' and these are the words I found; *recover, repair, restore (to life), retrieve, revive, repent*. The word 'Repent' especially, have a meaning that is totally different from its common usage and how most people understand it. Splitting the word 'repent' into two gives you 're' and 'pent'. The preface 're' usually refers to the act of getting something back which use to be missing from where it is supposed to be. The second part of the word is 'pent', which in building terminology usually refers to the topmost part of tall buildings. Hence putting the two phrases together, 'repent' would mean 'returning to the topmost position or level'. Therefore, when one is asked to repent, it is simply an instruction for them to return to the topmost part of life, which part can only be found when one's life is in alignment with the Lord Jesus Christ and the word of God. Hence, the next time you are instructed during a church service to 'repent' do not take offense to it as some do, thinking they are being picked-on. Interesting enough, to be instructed to repent is in your best interest since when you obey, repentance re-position you in the right place where you ought to be with God. Life in Christ is not a 'low-life'. It is life on a higher level than the standards of life based on the systems of this world.

In the early church, one was considered a member of the church, and one was a Christian, who had these three marks of distinction:

1. *One was baptized in the Name of Jesus for the remission of his sins in water;*
2. *One was baptized in the Holy Spirit; and*
3. *One called Jesus Lord.*

That was the sign of the ordinary early church Christian just about the days of the Apostles. They were baptized in water in the Name of the Lord Jesus for the remission of sins, acknowledging Christ as Lord by being baptized in water for remission of sins; and baptized in the Holy Ghost—real, true experience of New Birth Christianity. And the third one, where Jesus was Lord in everything, meant they were sanctified Christians who had Christ as the center of their lives.

Needed: Latter Rain Revival

See how things have changed today. For most part, today's church has lost the immanence of the Holy Ghost.

- *We acknowledge the Holy spirit as inspiring the Bible.*
- *We feel that the holy spirit occasionally inspires the preacher.*
- *-We feel also that the holy spirit inspires the choruses and hymns that we* sing

> *What we have lost is the personal touch or presence of the Holy Ghost amid His people, ruling, governing, and directing us. We seem to have forgotten that "as many as are led by the Spirit of God, the same are the sons of God".*

So the church of today has down-played the 'leading of the Spirit' in most of what we do on daily basis. For example, many born-again believers don't pray before they start their day anymore. They just jump from bed in the morning and begin a day that they know nothing about. Beginning your day without first spending time with the Lord for guidance is taking a great risk. It is a gamble, yet that's the norm for many believers because of how busy life has become for many.

The nearness, or the indwelling of God amongst His people is what is referred to as the *'immanence'*. That is what happens in revivals. And that is what God means by latter rain. That's what Joel says God will restore- the latter rain and He will come *in the midst of you*. I will dwell in the midst. What do we know today of the Holy Spirit being in our midst in the church? - very little, I guess or nothing at all. We long for and need revival. It's the latter rain. As the word of the Lord says, but how prepared is the church for this outpouring?

> **"I will give you the latter rain abundantly. And the floor shall be full of wheat. And the vat shall overflow with wine and oil…. And ye shall know that I am in the midst of Israel, and that I am the Lord your God, and none else. And my people shall never be ashamed. Joel 2:24, 27**

So, one of the greatest signs of revival is when the church knows and experienced without a shadow of doubt that the presence of God or the nearness of God is in their midst.

> ## *The nearness, or the indwelling of God amongst His people is what is referred to as the 'immanence'.*

This has nothing to do with the shouts, and singing, and hypes that we witness in most churches and that seem to be taking over the actual meaning of the presence of God in the midst of his people. This has nothing to do with the number of people in attendance on a particular Sunday or a count of how many people got baptized in water or even filled with the Holy Ghost. This is just the raw presence of God that cannot be ignored, disputed, or duplicated. This brings the individual to the place of wanting, yarning and desiring personal closeness with God. This is what is referred to as the 'nearness of God'. That is the product of revival and that is what true revivals brings to the church and into the life of the individual Christian. True revival is when the fear of God comes upon believers and unbelievers alike. It is when the nearness of God presence is felt by believers and unbelievers alike.

This is when the church is engulfed in his presence to such an extent that only God becomes our focus and desire. True revival not for the church alone. It is also a sign for the 'unchurched'. It is the place of the altar where God begins to make inquisition of truth into the lives of individuals and congregations alike. It is the place of spiritual transparency brought about by the spirit of God. The bible declares that the Spirit knoweth all things and search all things. True revival is bloody because it is the place where self is slain and the spirit of God is made alive in the life of an individual and the church as a whole. True revival is when the light of God's glory aglow in the life of the Church as a corporate body and the believer alike. Again, true revival is bloody to say the least.

When King David was bringing the ark of the covenant back to Jerusalem because they had not enquired of the Lord in the days of King Saul, notice that on their way to bring the ark back to Israel, there were lots of shouts, singing and dancing. Yet Uzza was strike dead from the experience, because the people weren't really prepared for a true revival. And if I may ask the question. Where did this breach come upon King David and the people. It occurred at a place called the 'threshing floor of Nachon'. The word 'Nachon' means preparation. Meaning that there was not enough preparation done to harbor the presence of God hence God brought judgement upon the occasion.

The next time around, in an attempt to transport the ark in the right way, the road that led from where the ark was located in the house of Obed Edom to Jerusalem became a bloody road as a result of the numerous sacrifices that were made as part of the spiritual protocol to transport the ark. The bible specifically stated that "so it was that after they that carried the ark had gone every five pace, that oxen and other animals were sacrificed as part of the protocol to transport the ark. Meanwhile nothing of that nature was done the first time they attempted to transport the ark. The reason, simply being that they were not prepared. They went for the ark only through excitement that it belongs to Israel and that it ought to come back to the place where it belong.

Cautionary Measures for Revival

If God begin to make inquisition of truth, where would we stand as a church? In the days of the early church the Lord could announce, *"I am He that walketh in the midst of the seven golden lampstands"* **[Revelation 2:1].**

But it doesn't seem like He walk in our midst so much today. Perhaps it's just as well He doesn't. If He did, the Ananias and Sapphira's among us who have found safe habitations in the church would drop dead again for lying to the Holy Ghost [Acts 5:1-11].

If the Spirit of God begin to make inquisitions into the truth, perhaps the 'Dathan' and 'Abiram' who have no regards for spiritual authority would be swallowed up into the belly of the earth as it did happen at the time of Moses. If the Spirit of God begin to make inquisitions into the truth, perhaps the 'Simon the Sorcerers' in the church who tries to manipulate the affairs of the church through their financial or social status would be cursed as in the days of the apostle Peter in Acts 8:9-24.

If God begin to make inquisition of truth, where would you stand as a believer in Christ? Be careful when you pray that the Holy Spirit should come back in immanence because the Spirit of truth won't walk amongst us unless He can walk in truth. And when He comes back, He must remove all the clutter and the untruth that we've filled up His church with. In the introductory chapters of the book of Revelation, notice that the glorified Lord walked in the midst of the seven golden lampstands, and because He did that, He could say to the Church in Ephesus; ***"I will remove your lampstand from its place"*** **[Revelation 2:5]**

And as a matter of fact, history tells us that He did remove their lampstand from its place. The Lord spoke to the church at Ephesus all the time the Apostle Paul was calling them back to His love. Later Jesus says to the Ephesians, *"You're right in your doctrine. And you know those who are possessors of truth and those who don't live it."* And although they had sorted all that out, yet they had left their first love says the spirit to the church in Ephesus. And because of that their lampstand was removed from its place. As a result of this word of prophecy to the church in Ephesus, today there is no church at modern day Ephesus at all. It is a totally deserted landscape in modern day country of Turkey. Interesting enough there is one at Smyrna (modern day city of Izmir in the country of Turkey), but not one in Ephesus, because the Lord always does what He says he will do. We want the Lord to come back and give us abundant showers of latter rain, but He comes along with the *immanence*, the personal touch, attention and standing of the Holy Spirit among God's people.

Mowed Grass

The promise of the Lord given in Psalm 72:6—says.

"He shall come down like rain upon the mown grass."

What is the grass that God is referring to? To give you a clue, it is what Isaiah says in chapter 40:6. When the voice said, *"Cry," he said, what shall I cry? And God said, Cry, All flesh is grass."*

Now link that, with Psalm 72:6 which says He will come down like showers upon the mown grass (flesh of men.) and like the grass that's cut down. What is the grass that's cut down? It's when we are willing to be cut down to size. It is when our puff-ups and arrogance is gone. It is when our prejudice against other Christians who don't have the same level of truth in God's words is gone and we are truly humble and can take correction in humility. It is when the Lord brings us down in humility and we can walk before the Lord in humbleness of heart and not in pomp, pride, and boastfulness of our abilities. It is when we realized that our own righteousness is as filthy rags before the Lord [Isaiah 64:6] and we realize that we have no power within us to help ourselves but rather all power comes from above. It is when we realize that any good that we do must be done by the Lord Jesus through us and that we are unprofitable servants even when we have done what He has told us to do [Luke 17:10]. That's the Lord cutting us down to size. That's the Lord coming down on the mown grass.

> **The Lord has promised to send the latter rain, his glorious latter rain of Holy Spirit anointing upon all flesh (grass), but it's imperative that the grass must first be mown.**

Surely the people are grass, says Isaiah, ***surely the people is grass. The grass withereth, and the flower fadeth, when the Spirit of the Lord bloweth upon it*** **[Isaiah 40:6-8]**

The implication here is that;

1) *you can either be withered by the Spirit of God*
2) *or you can be mown (humbled) and the Spirit of God will come upon you as refreshing and latter rain.*

When the Lord Jesus comes, He comes in judgment as well as in mercy. So, get your house in order. Get things right with God. Ask Him to give you a pure heart. Ask Him that you may be humble and mowed down instead of wither and die spiritually. The Lord loves to take little nothings and use them for His glory. He loves to announce that a worm shall thresh the mountains. It's unthought of to have a worm threshing the mountains! but that's what the Lord said He is going to do with those who submit to his perfect will.

76

"Fear not, thou worm Jacob...thou shall thresh the mountains, and beat them small..."Isaiah 41:14-15

But it's only God's worms that can do it. Ask the Lord to make you humble. Desire humility and the Lord will fulfill it in your life and after that shall the Lord bless you.

Blest are the humble souls that see
Their emptiness and poverty.
Treasures of grace to them are given
And crowns of joy laid up in heaven.
Blest are the men of broken heart
Who mourn for sin with inward smart.
They shall be divinely fed
On living streams and living bread.

It's what God wants you to pray and ask
for, in the words of Isaac Watts.
"...But for the Showers We Plead"

The Lord said, *"I will pour out My Spirit, in the last days, on all flesh."* This, He began at Pentecost. But that was only a minor beginning. Before the Lord Jesus comes back, the Holy Spirit is going to step back into the church in immanence, in power, and in His glory, and He is going to prepare the church for the coming of the Lord Jesus because the Lord is not coming for a defeated church. He is not coming for a church that is still struggling with sins. He is coming for a church without spot nor wrinkle the bible says. And then will come that Blessed One to reap His harvest, having abundantly refreshed the church, filled those ears of corn, and prepared for a most abundant and glorious harvest. O' What a glorious day and harvest that will be!

This will be the days when you will find that the things of the earth will grow strangely dim before you. You'll be able to drop them out of your hands without regret and out of your soul without yarning for their presence in your life ever again because you are looking for the coming of the Blessed One, the Most High God, the only King of the world and savior of mankind – Jesus is His name.

CHAPTER 8

WHY REVIVAL TARRIES

Many are those who would tell you and make you feel like the reason why revival tarries are all our fault or the fault of the church: and they would say things like; "it's because the believer and the church as a whole are not praying enough, fasting enough or not doing enough of one thing or the other." Or that America as a country is not praying enough that's why we are not seeing much revival, but that's not true either. The Most-high God sends revival in His will and in His time and not ours. He does it in His time and not when we feel like it should happen. God has great compassion towards His children. He listens to your prayers as if you are the only person in the whole world praying to Him. That might seem impossible to you but to God nothing is impossible.

You could not have an audience with the Queen of England even if you want to or the President of the United States in your lifetime; but isn't it a privilege that we tiny little creatures walking on two little legs upon the surface of God's vast universes can approach the Almighty God at any time be it mid-night, noon, or day and be heard.

> *It is worth noting that none of our prayers, efforts, programs, and groaning can ever push the hand of God to bring revival if the Spirit of God is not ready. We must understand that revival is God-sent not man-sent.*

A lot of things that's labelled as revival in the church today are only to gratify the flesh. Revival is literally God visiting His people and stepping into the realm of flesh. It is God, stepping into the sphere of humanity and making himself know in whichever way He pleases and chooses to reveal himself. Therefore, what we must do as Sons and Daughters of His Kingdom is to come to terms with the sovereignty of God. That is, whether revival is going to come to us or not, absolutely depends on the perfect counsel and will of God and very little or none of our doings. Although there are some human elements like true repentance that often triggers revivals, yet it is still up to God to decide the time of His visitation.

John 3:16 says; *"for God so loved the world that he gave His only begotten son."*

However, that's not the end of the redemption story because Christ also loved the church and gave Himself a ransom for it. Hence, there were two sacrifices at Calvary that blended into one

1) The sacrifice of the Father by giving His only begotten Son
2) And, the sacrifice of the Son, by laying down His life as a ransom for the Church.

It's therefore worth noting that God is deeply concern about the church of His dear son than we do or could ever do. He yarns over it just as His son Jesus Christ yarns over it. When the church lacks and needs revival, the Father knows, and He will give revival not in our time but His time because He makes all things beautiful only in His time.

> *The idea that God will hear because we have been asking for a very long time or that multitudes are asking Him at the same time, is an insult to God's majesty because God is not moved by time nor by number.*

God will choose to do what He plans to do by few or by many regardless.

The Church belongs to His beloved and dear Son and so if we as men are concern about the church it means He is even more concern about it than us. However, the questions we ought to be asking ourselves are,

- *when would the father send revival.*
- *will we be ready when He sends revival*
- *how long will it take for Him to visit His people, and*
- *why the long gaps between major revivals?*

The Charismatic renewal movement that swept through America and other parts of the world in the decades of the 1980s and 1990s was not really a revival in the true sense and meaning of the word. It just served the purpose it was send and meant to serve, which is, to break barriers between the various denominations. That's why today, we have Holy Ghost filled Baptist, Lutherans, Presbyterians etc. The Charismatic renewal was not a revival because the two main components or ingredients of a true revival were not present.

1) *A burning concern for holiness*
2) *Passionate confession of sins the leads to true repentance were both missing.*

That's why today, it's all gone into the shadows. So, you may be wondering; if God truly loves us, then why? Why has He tarry so long.? I would like to spend some time to engage you in the understanding God has given me of why revival tarries.

WHY DO REVIVAL TARRY?

There are a couple of different theological opinions from different schools of thought as to why the occurrence of revivals tarry. I want to share what my convictions are on this subject with you as to why I believe revivals tarry at times.

There are two great principles that God works on.

1) The Lord will do nothing except He reveal it to His servants the prophets. (God speaking to us through His servant)
2) I would yet be inquired of, to do it for them.

Ezekiel. 36:37

> *"Thus, saith the Lord God; I will yet for this be enquired of by the house of Israel, to do it for them; I will increase them with men like a flock."*

Since the Lord's return will be for a church without spots and wrinkles, it implies there ought to be some level of purging before the Lord's advent. Hence before the Lord comes for His church, His Holy Spirit will have to step into his church to purge it and make it ready for the holy bride. Hence the statement.

*"The Lord will come **to** His church before He come **for** His church."*

When He comes **to** His church, it will be by the Holy Spirit but when He comes **for** His Church, He is coming in the person of the glorified Lord and Savior Jesus Christ.

Hence as simple as the two prepositions 'to' and 'for' are, they make a big difference in the agenda of God for the church. This is because of the relationship between Christ and His church is that the church is the Bride of Christ. Therefore, for Him to come *for* His church, He must first prepare the bride to be without spot nor wrinkle just like the brides were prepared for months and at times years to make them ready for their groom in the days of old. Esther and the other maidens were prepared for at least six months before they could have a moment before the King. If that extent of preparation was deemed necessary for the brides of earthly kings, then what about Jesus who is the King of Kings and the Lord of Lords. Don't you think an even much more preparations will be needed for His coming. For the Church, the work of preparation and regeneration, however, will be done by His Holy Spirit.

Why are there gaps in revivals then?

Consider the following notable but much recent revivals of the past decades and century.

Azusa Street revival-1906

The Hebrides Island Revival- 1949

The Pensacola Revival- 1995

> *The history of the New Testament church as well as revivals of modern times teaches us that there have always been gaps of years before the Lord send revivals.*

The answer to "why it takes long to get revivals going" is in the following statement. How long does it take to get a flock of sheep together? – very little time. But how long does it take to produce Shepherds? – A lifetime isn't it.? Therefore, God could produce a nation in a day and multitudes of sheep overnight because with time we are all His sheep. Remember Jesus' statement that God could raise stones to worship Him if men refuses to do so. The issue therefore is not the bringing together of the flock but rather it is in the making of good Shepherds who are capable of taking care of the flock of God. God needs Shepherds to look after the sheep hence He can't produce sheep when there are no committed Shepherds to look after the sheep. The Shepherds help to keep the sheep from going astray; the Shepherds have burden for the sheep. They take time to cater for the spiritual needs of the sheep. All we like sheep has gone astray: we have done those things we need not do, and it seem there are not enough good and committed Shepherds to guide us back on track.

God could produce sheep in revivals so easily, but He is also concern about putting the sheep in the hands of good and faithful Shepherds for the sheep to grow.

So, in brief, it takes gaps in-between revivals because it takes time for God to prepare the Shepherds before He produces the sheep. The word Shepherd in the Greek is 'pastor', but it does not mean only pastors are Shepherds. The reason God is instructing you in the word and grooming you in His church is so when revival comes, you will be able to Shepherd other sheep that will be produce as a result of the revival. That said, take in all the word you can and prepare yourself for what lies ahead on God's agenda for His church because there is a sound of abundance of rain (both the former rains and the latter rains together), but it's going to need more hands than you ever imagine to cater for the sheep that are going to be birth as a result of the outpouring of the former and latter rains together in these end times.

> *When revival comes, you wouldn't have to ask people to come to church; you wouldn't have to go knocking from door-to-door because the people themselves are going to find their way into God's presence*

True revival is literally like when the church or the body of Christ reaches a point after being in constant repentance and prayer and God steps in to say; *"you have prayed enough; you just leave the rest in my hands to do and then God goes on to take care of His business in an unprecedented way".* Just like it happened in the book of Acts -sinners will find their way into the church and say, **"what must we do to be saved"** and the reason why they would come to you is because they see in you, or in the church, what they have been looking for.

During the series of revivals that hit the Hebrides Islands in Scotland in the late 1940's, so much conviction came upon the people of the Islands such that it was said on one occasion that in the middle of the night people couldn't have peaceful sleep in their homes. According to accounts from eyewitnesses, people started gathering at the Police Precinct because they came to the consciousness that something was wrong with their heart, but they didn't know exactly what it was. Therefore, in their ignorance and not knowing what to do with the guilt and conviction they felt, they started to gather in front of the police precinct in the middle of the night to check themselves in to the police as wrong doers although they had not committed any civil crimes. That is what true revival can do to the conscience of the sinner and the sinful world around us. I will show you in the next chapter, from scripture how God takes the trouble to produce Shepherds beginning with Abraham.

CHAPTER 9

SHEPHERDING HEART: A PREREQUISITE FOR REVIVAL

Abraham:

God called Abraham from the East. Pulled him out from his father's household in the Ur of the Chaldees and he went by the banks of the Euphrates River because he was a Shepherd and could find water for his flock along the river. In the process of time came his son Isaac who was not a Shepherd and hence notice that God's dealings with Isaac was very limited. We did not hear much in the bible about Isaac and his relationship with God as we did about Abraham and Isaac's son Jacob. Because of that God had to sort of by-pass Isaac and to raise up another Shepherd in the person of Isaac's son Jacob. Jacob we all know became the founder of the nation of Israel, and a Shepherd of renown. The same applies to Moses, who became the great leader of the nation Israel. He was learned in all the wisdom of the Egyptians the bible says, and one would think that all the great leadership skills acquired from the

Palace of Pharaoh which was then the pivotal center of the world's civilization, would be more than enough for God to make Moses lead His people. But God proved to us through the life of Moses that He doesn't care what knowledge or education one may have had before coming to him. God must first develop you into a Shepherd before He can use you to lead his sheep.

I have had personal experiences of my own that I can share with you when it comes to God's preparations in the making of a Shepherd. One of the areas in my life that I did struggle with was anger. But God had to deal with me on that and turned me around in order to be able to begin His journey with me as one of His Under-Shepherds. You may be surprised to hear this testimony if you happen to know me today, but for those closer to me who had knew me all along, they will tell you that I have indeed come a long way from where I use to be as far as with anger and sharp temper is concern.

God took Moses out of Egypt and for 40 years he attended to the sheep of his father-in-law Jethro. Forty years, like 40 days symbolizes testing. Remember Jesus was tested after being in obsolesce through prayer and fasting for forty days. Israel was also tested in the wilderness for forty years, so forty is the number or symbol of testing.

In the twenty-first chapter of the gospel of John, Jesus asked Peter a question that Peter found to be troubling, not at the first time but by the fact that Jesus repeated the same question thrice.

> ***John 21:15-17*** *[15] So when they had dined, Jesus saith to Simon Peter, Simon,*

son of Jonas, lovest thou me more than these? He saith unto him, Yea, Lord; thou knowest that I love thee. He saith unto him, Feed my lambs.

[16] He saith to him again the second time, Simon, son of Jonas, lovest thou me? He saith unto him, Yea, Lord; thou knowest that I love thee. He saith unto him, Feed my sheep.

[17] He saith unto him the third time, Simon, son of Jonas, lovest thou me? Peter was grieved because he said unto him the third time, Lovest thou me? And he said unto him, Lord, thou knowest all things; thou knowest that I love thee. Jesus saith unto him, Feed my sheep.

Jesus ask Peter "do you love me" three times and when Peter responded with a resounding 'yes' Jesus then instructed him to feed his lamb. But notice that after questioning Peter again for a second and a third time, Jesus' instruction to Peter was a little different. On the second and third occasions, Jesus said to Peter; if you love me, keep my sheep (not lamb). The difference between the first instruction and the second and third can be found in Jesus' use of the words *Lamb* and *Sheep*. The interesting implication I see here is that God would not allow you to keep his sheep (flock) until you have learnt to keep his Lamb. A lamb is the young of a sheep, while the sheep is usually used in the sense of a 'flock'. Hence, no matter how much you pray and fast for God to put into your hands the care of His flock, God will not honor such prayers until you have learnt to deal with your brother and sister and also the new converts who represent the lamb among God's flock.

David:

Now consider King David whom God choose as a successor of King Saul, to be the new King of the nation Israel. God first trained him to be a Shepherd, so he could Shepherd God's people one day. However, Solomon; his Son and successor, was not a Shepherd so when you investigate the lives of the two men (Father and Son), you would find out that they totally differ in the way they handled the people under their care and those they disagreed with.

> *While Solomon was quick to put to death his enemies and rivals, David was far more patient in handling people who offended him or disagreed with him because of the shepherding qualities in David.*

At one time during what will be the greatest agony of his life, David while on the run from his favorite son

Absalom during the revolt of Absalom to take over the Kingdom from his father, came to a place called *Bahurim* where he met a man by named *Shimei* (a Benjamite, from the House of Saul). Without any provocation, Shimei began to curse out at David and throw stones at the King. The men with David could have killed *Shimei* in a matter of seconds but look at what David's respond was to this unruly man as recorded in II Sam 16:5-11(READ)

2 Samuel 16:5-10 (KJV)

"And when king David came to Bahurim, behold, thence came out a man of the family of the house of Saul, whose name was Shimei, the son of Gera: he came forth, and cursed still as he came. [6] And he cast stones at David, and at all the servants of king David: and all the people and all the mighty men were on his right hand and on his left. [7] And thus said Shimei when he cursed, come out, come out, thou bloody man, and thou man of Belial: [8] The Lord hath returned upon thee all the blood of the house of Saul, in whose stead thou hast reigned; and the Lord hath delivered the kingdom into the hand of Absalom thy son: and behold, thou art taken in thy mischief, because thou art a bloody man. [9] Then said Abishai the son of Zeruiah unto the king, why should this dead dog curse my lord the king? let me go over, I pray thee, and take off his

head. [10] And the king said, what have I to do with you, ye sons of Zeruiah? so let him curse, because the Lord hath said unto him, Curse David. Who shall then say, wherefore hast thou done so?

Shimei's head would have been long gone off the rest of his body if he was to behave in such a manner towards King Solomon, but he got away with such an ill behavior towards David because David had the patience of a Shepherd in his dealing with people. It is my earnest prayer that God will give us the heart and spirit of a Shepherd whether we are called to be Pastors in the Kingdom of God or to serve in some other capacity because it will take the heart of a Shepherd to keep the flock of God together. Whiles hot-tempered men and women who lack self-control scatters the flock, it takes men and women with the spirit of a Shepherd to keep the flock of God together.

God only uses people with Shepherding hearts to lead His people and He is working on your life right now to turn you into a good Shepherd in preparation towards the end-time revival that He is about to unleash upon His church universal.

> **You don't have to be ordained a pastor or have the title (Rev) before your name to be one of those good Shepherds that God is preparing for the end–time harvest of souls. God is seeking for a willing and obedient heart to use for His purposes.**

The title 'Reverend' that many are dying to have in front of their names, is not what makes one a Shepherd. I have come across people in the church who get offended when you don't address them by certain titles. These days people are clamoring for titles whiles ignoring the actual functions and responsibilities that goes along with the titles. The title "*Rev*"- may only give you some sort of standing with the government so you can perform marriages or officiate other clerical duties, however that is not what qualifies you as a Shepherd after God's own heart. God cares so much about the making and quality of his Shepherds that he promises in his word to give His people Shepherds after his own heart and not after the desires of men.

Jeremiah 3:14–15

> *"Return, unfaithful people,[a] declares the* LORD, *for I am your husband.[b] I'll take you, one from a city and two from a family, and I'll bring you to Zion. 15 I'll give you shepherds[c] after my own heart, and they'll shepherd you with knowledge and good sense."*

You must have the inward calling and Spirit of God upon your life for God to make you one of his good shepherds. That's what makes one God's shepherd not the mere letters in a clerical title.

> *True revival is already happening around the globe in these last days, however what's being experienced are only sporadic proportions of the great out-pouring of His Spirit.*

God want to prepare us as shepherds first before He sends out both the former and the latter rains of revival together upon His church.

Great revivals always begin with dedication to constant and perpetual prayer of the church. Before the Hebrides Island revival was birth: God first put the burden on the heart of two elderly ladies (one named Peggy Smith), and for years they met to pray in an old barn for God to bring a revival because the younger generation on the Island weren't going to church anymore. Whiles the night clubs and the cinema halls were rather packed to capacity on Saturday nights with young people, pews in the churches were empty on Sunday mornings. After years of praying and seeking God, revival finally broke out but there were no shepherds to direct and lead the revival on the Island. The two old ladies therefore prayed for God to bring a minister who speaks their language to lead the revival. The Lord answered their prayer and spoke to a Minister by name Duncan Campbell to go down to the Islands to lead the revival that had just started.

Although God gave Abraham a promise of a great nation through his seed, his son Isaac couldn't lead the nation God wanted to give birth to because he was not a shepherd. As a matter of fact, Isaac cared about his stomach more than he could ever care about a flock. It was Isaac who said, ***"I am dying so bring me my favorite food that I may eat so my soul would bless you"***.

Why would a dying man care so much about food before he dies? Most people when dying, cares for more time to live in order to accomplish things they had plans of accomplishing in the future. But for Isaac, he seem to care more about that special food than for more time to live. That sound like some church folks and some church fellowship meeting isn't it- is all about food. So, it is worth noting that Isaac's blessings to his sons were through food and not through faith. Meanwhile his son Jacob, at the point of death, never asked for food in order to bless what would become the twelve great tribes of Israel. This is because he had the heart of a shepherd.

Then Isaac said, *" I know not the day of my death"* and he lived only to died 20 years after that statement. So, he literally lived the last 20 years of his life preparing to die and did not die until the space of 20 more years. That's certainly not the way I want to die. I want to live every moment of my life fully until I take my last breath out of this world. I don't want to spend 20 years of my limited life concentrating on dying and planning for death whiles I'm still alive – that's certainly not wisdom.

Isaac was certainly not God's shepherd to produce the kind of nation God wanted hence God had to bypass him and choose Jacob His Son. Therefore, notice that Jacob owned nothing when he left home although his grandfather Abraham did. Both his father and grandfather were both exceedingly rich in lands and in cattle. God started with Jacob from the scratch I would say. He started life with nothing and through the process of time God prepared him as a shepherd after His own heart. That's why Jacob could say: in Gen 32:10 *"for with my staff I passed over this Jordan; and now I am become two bands."*
Genesis 31:40–41 (KJV)

> *"Thus I was; in the day the drought consumed me, and the frost by night; and my sleep departed from mine eyes. [41] Thus have I been twenty years in thy*

house; I served thee fourteen years for thy two daughters, and six years for thy cattle: and thou hast changed my wages ten times".

Jacob started life as a man of guile, but God turned Jacob the man of guile into a man of God. Jacob the supplanter, was now suffering deception from the hand of Laban. In like manner, Jesus spoke to Nathaniel later and said *"Behold and Israelite indeed in whom there is no guile"*; but wait a minute; wasn't the father of the nation Israel (Jacob) a guileful man, one may ask. Yes, that's true but God had to turn him around before he made him into a nation. If God could do that for Jacob, then there is hope for anyone of us isn't it? Jacob was a man of guile but his encounter with God, changed him into a man without

Whenever one truly encounters God in their life, God always leaves a mark on them. It may not be a physical mark as in the case of Jacob, but there will always be an indelible spiritual mark of some sort when that encounters occurs.

guile. During that encounter, God left a mark on Jacob for the rest of his life. Jacob left the presence of God with a limp, which is something that would stay with him for the rest of his life.

Years after my walk with the Lord, it happened to me and I knew it without a shadow of doubt that something had shifted spiritually in my relationship with God. The things that use to easily entice my attention, became powerless in my presence and the power of some desires that I struggled with for years dissipated like a vapor before my very eyes. To me, that encounter with God felt like I was already living in the millennium years of glory where the lion and the lamb will dwell together in harmony without one devouring the other.

For Jacob, it was better for the sun to rise upon a limping Israel than to set upon a guileful Jacob. It was better for him to walk away from this divine encounter with a limping leg than to walk away unchanged. Therefore this is what happens to a man or a woman when they truly encounters God.

1) *God leaves an indelible mark upon their lives. (And if you were to ask Jacob why he limped: he would say well God touch me, and he left a mark on me)*
2) *God changes their name and gives them a new name.*
3) *The indelible mark and the change of name leads to a change in their destiny.*

As a result of that divine encounter with God in the form of an angel, Jacob's name was changed to Israel meaning a Prince of God. Abraham was Abram (High father), but God changed his name to Abraham (Father of multitudes). Isaac's name means laughter and he never got a change in his name, and what a difference in the end of Jacob's life as compared to Isaac his father. From the lives of these two men, I found out that one can have grace to live which is called a living grace, however, I also found out that one can have dying grace such that when their time comes to depart from this earth, God will see them through their exit from this earth graciously.

At the end of his life, Isaac asked for his favorite food to eat first before he gives His blessing to his eldest son. Thinking he was about to die soon, he ended up living for another 20 years. I don't know what I would be doing with myself if I had to live the last 20 years of my life just preparing to die. This is exactly what happens to many people after they have declared themselves as 'retirees. For many, they literally live the rest of their life trying hard to slow down their lives so they will fit into a social profile or group called 'Retired Persons of America' (RPA), while lingering and waiting for the eventual end of their exit from this life.

I learnt some time ago that there is no such word as 'retirement' in the Hebrew. According to ancient Jewish wisdom, when there is no word for a particular thing, it implies that thing does not exist. Hence, since there is no word for retirement in the Hebrew, it implies that retirement is simply someone's idea of how their physical life on this earth should end. That may not necessarily be God's ideal for our lives. Notice in the bible that none of the Patriarchs or the faithful retired from their service unto God until the very moment they took their last breath, and that is what I look forward to in my life. While I will train and mentor successors, I do not intend to withdraw myself from God's service until the day he gives me grace to die.

Unlike his father Isaac, Jacob towards the end of his life when he was about to die and while leaning on a rod did not ask for Joseph or any of his other eleven sons to bring him his favorite dish so he could eat to bless them. On the contrary, at the time of his nearness to death, Jacob had already blessed Pharaoh. He had already blessed his twelve children and in addition to that, he had also blessed the two sons of Joseph – Ephraim and Manasseh.

But watch what he did although the bible says his eyes were dim. Joseph placed Manasseh (the elder son) on Jacob's right hand to have the greater blessing and Ephraim the younger on Jacobs left hand for the lesser blessings. Although Jacob couldn't see them well because his eyes were deem but by faith and contrary to the traditions of the day, he crossed his hands so his right hand will be upon the younger son Ephraim to impart a greater blessing and his left hand upon Manasseh (the older) to impart a lesser blessing. What a difference that makes with Jacob as compared to his father Isaac who couldn't bless unless his stomach is full of his favorite dish. What a difference the spiritual man is from the canal. Joseph said to his father Jacob; it's not so father, you have blessed the young above the older and Jacob said in response, I know my son, I know.

It is worth noting that some of us are who we are today and where we are today because contrary to the wishes of the devil, God crossed His hands over us. Some of us are in our right minds today because God decided to cross His hands over our lives. Some are still alive today because the Almighty God decided to change our destiny although the demands of traditions of men and the systems of this world would not permit for you to go any further than your eyes can see. This is just like what King Solomon said, The Lord brought us to the banqueting house and guess what else the Lord did? the banner he raised over us has in its L-O-V-E (love).

> *"He brought me to the banqueting house, and his banner over me was love"*
> **(Songs of Solomon 2:4)**

I'm so glad Jesus is not only coming *for* his church soon, but he is going to come *to* his church through the Holy Ghost before He comes for His Church. That's why I know from scripture and I'm very confident that there is going to be a mighty outpouring of the Holy Ghost power and revival in these end times. The reason why God must take you through disappointments, pain and suffering is because He is preparing you to be his shepherd. That's why you are not liked by many. That's why many of your former friends has turn their backs at you. That's why you are hated by some, and things are being said about you that is false.

God will take you through some deep soul-searching agonies just so he will prepare you to be one of the good shepherds He is preparing and putting together for a mighty outpouring of both the former and latter rains of end-time revival. Isaiah 37:3 says **".....for the children**

are come to the birth, and there is not strength to bring forth. May it never be said of the church of today, that we came to the point of birth (revival) and did not have the strength to bring forth the will of God for our lives, our church and our generation.

APPENDIX 1

AUDIO TAPES BY THE AUTHOR

There are 3 phases to freedom. Bondage, Deliverance and Change in Mindset. Deliverance is not the same thing as Freedom because while deliverance is instantaneous, freedom is a process. Strikingly and interestingly, the Nation of Israel, Our Lord Jesus Christ, as well as every New Testament Believer, started their journey of faith from Egypt (Bondage).

- We all must go through our first body of water (Red Sea)
- We all must go through our share of trials & temptations (Wilderness)
- We all must cross our second body of water (Jordan)
- But not all will be able to get to the promise land of Canaan (Freedom)

The 4 Degrees of Relationship, Friends; Choose godly, choose wisely. (Part 1-7)

We all have some form of associations within our sphere of life. Our success or failure in life hangs strongly on the nature of our associations. In this 7 part teaching series Dr. Nyarko expounds on the key ingredients to a wise, healthy and godly relationship using the example of Jesus as our model. Dr. Nyarko's approach to this subject will leave you amused, instructed, enlightened, stirred up, and challenged but definitely not bored.

Understanding Kingdom Authority (Part 1-3)

Many folks in church know that there is power in the blood of Jesus only a few knows how this power goes to work for humanity. In this 3-part series audio tape, you will be blown away by the in-depth teachings by Dr. Nyarko on the Blood of Jesus and why he is referred to as the Lamb of God.

WHILE MEN SLEPT. (Part 1 & 2)

This message depicts "A wild Bull caught in a net"
(Isaiah 52:20) which in a way, is the Portrait of a Sleeping Church which although has been endowed with great power yet ensnared by little things.

THE STATE OF SIN & THE ACT OF SIN

There is a striking difference between the state of sin and the act of sin. Here is a brief definition of the two. "All have sinned and come short the glory of God". That is the state of sin. But after salvation, the bible also says, "if we confess our sins, he is faithful and just to forgive and cleanse us from all unrighteousness". That is the act of Sin. How are they handled?

THE MANTLE & THE SPIRIT.

Elisha received a double portion of Elijah's anointing but what does this really mean? He received a mantle, and he also received a spirit transfer.

PRAYER: THE POWER OF PETITIONING (Parts 1-4)

The is the most exercised event of the church and yet the least understood act in the church. Prayer, for many has been turned into presenting a 'shopping list' to God. This series of messages on prayer deals with the legal grounds of what it means to present a petition to God.

This is a timely message of accountability for every Believer. God's prime purpose for creating man, according to the book of Genesis was to find a Manager for all His creation. Hence God will first test our trustworthiness before He entrust anything into our care. This is because to him the much is given, much shall be required, the bible says.

THE ACT OF WORSHIP

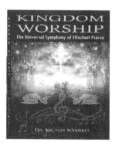

This 3 series tape will leave you amused and enlightened but not bored. It is an in-depth exposition of Psalm 149 and reveals how true worship should be in the sanctuary of our God based on the meaning of the common word Hallelujah. (Halal Yah)

The story of Job is one that is hard to comprehend with. It has more 'why' than answers. It always leads to the age-old question of "Why should the Righteous Suffer"? This series of tapes will bring answers as well as comfort to you in your moments of suffering. Listen to it and pass the message on.

Have you ever thought of the fact that God does not live in time but created time for man to live in.? Time is the most precious commodity that we have as humans. While we may have different ethnic backgrounds, may differ in knowledge, wealth, education etc., we are all given the same amount of time within each day. Therefore, what you end up becoming, is largely dependent on how you use your time. Time is too precious to waste so make sure you don't let it slip out of your hands unawares.

We are saved momentarily when we surrender our lives to Christ and accept His Lordship over our lives, however growing into perfection is not attained overnight. It is a gradual and progressive work of God that can only take place with the cooperation of an individual with the work of the Holy Spirit.

THE 7TH RESURRECTION.

This is an Easter message of hope both in the present and future for the child of God who looks to the saving power of the cross in his or her daily life. While it is true that Christ died and resurrected for the sake of sinful humanity, it is worth noting also that His death and especially his resurrection was the 7th resurrection account in the entire bible. It was the 7th because the number seven is a symbol of perfection, and His resurrection was meant to perfect all that had occurred before Him in that it was the only resurrection that served as the first fruit of all of them that died in the Lord.

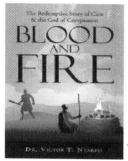

This book is about the biblical story of Cain and Abel, the first products of human procreation through Adam and Eve. This story is unique in that there are a couple of things done that were unknowns to human history. It is a story that although began with God's judgement against sinful human nature inherited through Adam and Eve, however, it ends with the powerful act of redemption that only comes from a God of second chances.

Printed in the United States
by Baker & Taylor Publisher Services